The Japanese Automobile Industry

Recent Titles in
Bibliographies and Indexes in Economics and Economic History

The Green Revolution: An International Bibliography
M. Bazlul Karim, compiler

Information for International Marketing: An Annotated Guide to Sources
James K. Weekly and Mary K. Cary, compilers

Telecommunication Economics and International Regulatory Policy: An Annotated
Bibliography
Marcellus S. Snow and Meheroo Jussawalla, compilers

Manpower for Energy Production: An International Guide to Sources with
Annotations
Djehane A. Hosni, compiler

Central European Economic History from Waterloo to OPEC, 1815-1975:
A Bibliography
Richard D. Hacken, compiler

International Real Estate Valuation, Investment, and Development
Valerie J. Nurcombe

Japanese Direct Foreign Investments: An Annotated Bibliography
Karl Boger, compiler

Economic Methodology: A Bibliography with References to Works in the
Philosophy of Science, 1860-1988
Deborah A. Redman, compiler

A Literature Guide to the Hospitality Industry
Philip Sawin, Denise Madland, Mary K. Richards, and Jana Reeg Steidinger,
compilers

Successful Industrial Product Innovation: An Integrative Literature Review
Roger J. Calantone and C. Anthony di Benedetto, compilers

The Social Dimensions of International Business: An Annotated Bibliography
Jon P. Alston, compiler

The Savings and Loan Crisis: An Annotated Bibliography
Pat L. Talley, compiler

THE JAPANESE AUTOMOBILE INDUSTRY

An Annotated Bibliography

Compiled by
SHEAU-YUEH J. CHAO

Bibliographies and Indexes in Economics and Economic History,
Number 15

GREENWOOD PRESS
Westport, Connecticut • London

Library of Congress Cataloging-in-Publication Data

Chao, Sheau-yueh J.
   The Japanese automobile industry : an annotated bibliography /
compiled by Sheau-yueh J. Chao.
      p.   cm.—(Bibliographies and indexes in economics and
economic history, ISSN 0749-1786 ; no. 15)
   Includes indexes.
   ISBN 0-313-28678-7 (alk. paper)
      1. Automobile industry and trade—Japan—Bibliography.   I. Title.
II. Series.
Z5170.C43   1994
[HD9710.J32]
016.3384'76292'0952—dc20   93-35797

British Library Cataloguing in Publication Data is available.

Library of Congress Catalog Card Number: 93-35797
ISBN: 0-313-28678-7
ISSN: 0749-1786

First published in 1994

Greenwood Press, 88 Post Road West, Westport, CT 06881
An imprint of Greenwood Publishing Group, Inc.

Printed in the United States of America

The paper used in this book complies with the
Permanent Paper Standard issued by the National
Information Standards Organization (Z39.48-1984).

10 9 8 7 6 5 4 3 2 1

Contents

Introduction

The Japanese automobile industry has risen from obscurity
to become the world's leading producer of automobiles in less
than 30 years. In 1960, Japan's total share of world output
for automobiles was only 1.27%, but by 1987 it had soared to
23.8%. The global share for the U.S. auto industry in the
same period fell from 51% in 1960 to 21.4% in 1987. Since
1980, Japan's automobile industry has emerged as the world's
leading global vehicle producer, outstripping the United
States. Recently, Japan has achieved a one-third share of the
American auto market. Its outreach strategy aiming at overseas
expansion was mainly focused on the United States, and in
recent years, the Japanese have also made inroads into the
markets of Asian and European countries. A success story in
the business world like the Japanese automobile industry will
certainly draw increasing interest among the general public as
well as researchers in this field.

Many current studies of the Japanese have been published
in subjects such as foreign investments, organizational
behavior, corporate management, economics, education, and
religion. Numerous articles in this field and the relatively
few books that have been published indicate the need for a
greater research effort, especially in the United States,
which receives a major portion of the Japanese investment.

So far, no extensive bibliographic research study has
concentrated solely on the Japanese automobile industry. This
bibliography is an attempt to fill the gap by compiling all
the substantial works in one single volume. All published
works were eligible for inclusion--books, articles,
bibliographies, encyclopedias, yearbooks, periodicals,
conference papers, government documents, monographs, and
audio-visual materials. Preference was, however, given to
articles in academic rather than popular journals.
Nevertheless, some articles of exceptional quality or
particular interest from popular journals have been included

as well. Also, in view of the different types of media
existing today, the volume covers audio-visual materials,
including a wide selection of video recordings, films, motion
pictures, and sound cassettes.

This annotated bibliography provides comprehensive
coverage of materials from the period between 1980 and 1992
and also includes particularly important works published
before 1980. It is limited to works in the English language
that address the situation of the Japanese automobile
industry, particularly as it relates to the U.S. automobile
industry.

The bibliography includes more than 600 annotated
citations. Part I covers books, documents, monographs, and
articles. Materials are divided into broad topical chapters
based on significant aspects of the subject matter. Part II
covers periodicals, bibliographies, encyclopedias, yearbooks,
other general reference works, and audio-visual aids. In each
chapter, citations are arranged in alphabetical order by
author or by title where no author is given, and a
chronological order is used for the list of works written by
one author. The volume opens with a list of abbreviations and
a chronology.

This bibliography focuses on the Japanese automobile
industry and industrial development in the postwar era,
especially the mass-expansion period from 1980 to the present.
It touches the following major subjects: the relationship of
the U.S. and Japanese auto industries; operation of the
Japanese transplants in the U.S.; case studies of major
Japanese auto manufacturers, including Toyota, Nissan,
Mitsubishi, Honda, Mazda, Isuzu, and Subaru; joint ventures
between United States and Japanese automakers; and government
trade issues, including rules and legislation for Japan's
export quotas.

The author, title, and subject indexes will facilitate
the use of this bibliography. Audio-visual materials are
identified in the title and subject indexes. Key words from
the title and its annotations are used as cross references.
Specific entries have been made in the indexes for geographic
names and corporate entities, especially in case studies and
comparative analyses of the United States and Japanese firms.
An attempt has been made to place material under the most
appropriate heading, but this is often ambiguous. It is hoped
the subject index will help correct this problem and make this
bibliography more accessible. In Part II, Chapter 8 of
Periodicals, an unknown publication date is marked as "u."
For example, "19uu-" means the title has been published since
1900s but the exact date is not known.

I wish to thank Professor Raymond Chang for his insight,
guidance, and suggestions throughout the project. I am also
grateful to my colleagues Eric Neubacher and Louisa Moy for
their interlibrary loan arrangements. Professor Kristin
McDonough, Professor Stanton Biddle, Professor Spencer Means,
and Mr. Steve Sacher provided editorial support for the book.
Finally, I wish to thank my husband, Eugene, for supporting

and encouraging my efforts throughout the compiling process for this book.

Abbreviations

CAFE
The U.S. law regulates auto fuel economy standards with an average number of miles per gallon of gasoline. The current "corporate average fuel economy" standard is 27.5 miles per gallon of gasoline, as of January 1992.

DSM
Diamond-Star Motors Corporation, a joint venture between Mitsubishi Motors Corporation and Chrysler Corporation built in Normal, Illinois, in 1988.

HAM
Honda of America Manufacturing Inc., built in 1979, in Marysville, Ohio. It was the first Japanese transplant and has been a pathfinder for other Japanese automobile manufacturers and suppliers.

HONDA
Japanese car and motorcycle line produced from 1967 to date by Honda Motor Co. Ltd. The company was founded in 1948 by Mr. Soichiro Honda. Popular U.S. car models include: Accord, Acura, CRX, Integra, Legend (an Acura model), NS-X (sports car), Prelude, and Civic.

ISUZU
Japanese car line produced from 1953 to date by Isuzu Motors Ltd. It entered the car business in 1938 as Ishikawajima Shipbuilding Company Ltd. The company name was changed to Isuzu Motors Ltd. in 1949. General Motors became part owner of the company in 1971. Popular U.S. car models include: I-Mark, Impulse (sports-car model), Rodeo (truck model) and Trooper (sports-utility model).

JAMA
Japan Automobile Manufacturers Association.

JAPIA   Japan Auto Parts Industry Association.

JETRO   Japan External Trade Organization.

JIDOKA   Establishing harmony (Wa) between people and
                machines in order to build in quality.

JIT   "Just-in-time," "Kanban" in Japanese; a
                manufacturing system based on the precise
                coordination and timing of parts, materials,
                and processes in the assembly room. Large
                inventories of parts are not required, as they
                are ordered directly from the parts suppliers
                as needed.

KAIZEN   "Constant improvement" in Japanese; the never-
                ending quest for the improvement of all
                aspects of the automaking business:
                production, management, engineering,
                manufacturing, and distribution.

KANBAN   See JIT.

KEIRETSU   "Group affiliation" in Japanese; the peculiar
                corporate relationships that exist in Japan,
                concerning a group of close-knit ties that buy
                from within the group rather than outside.

MAZDA   Japanese car line produced from 1920 to date
                by Mazda Motor Corporation. It was founded in
                1920 by Jujiro Matsudo as Toyo Kogyo which
                produces corks. The name changed to Toyo
                Kogyo Company Ltd. in 1927. The first Mazda
                car was produced in 1961 with the first rotary
                engine in 1967.   Popular U.S. car models
                include: Miata, MX-3, MX-6, MX-8, RX-7, 323,
                626, 929.

MITI   Japan's Ministry of International Trade and
                Industry.

MITSU-   Japanese car line produced from 1917 to 1921
BISHI   and from 1959 to date by Mitsubishi Motors
                Corp. Ltd. The company formed a joint venture
                with Chrysler Corp. in 1988 called Diamond-
                Star Motors Corp., in Normal, Illinois.
                Popular U.S. car models include: Colt (built
                in Japan for Dodge), Cordia, Diamonte, Galant,
                Mighty Max (truck model), Mirage, Montero,
                Precis, Sigma, Starion, and Tredia.

MMUC   Mazda Motor Manufacturing USA Corporation,
                established in 1987, in Flat Rock, Michigan.

NISSAN   Japanese car line produced from 1960 to date
                by Nissan Motor Co. Ltd.   The cars

manufactured by the company were called
"Datsun" because the company was formed by
three Japanese financiers: Den, Aoyama, and
Takeuchi. The company name was called Kai
Shinsha Motors in early 1930s. It was merged
with Kaishinsha Motor Car Works in 1933. The
company name was changed into Nissan Motor Co.
Ltd. in 1934. Nissan entered the American
auto market in 1958 with Datsun 310, now named
Bluebird. Cars were produced under the Datsun
label until early 1980s. Popular U.S. car
models include: 300 ZX (sports car), Altima,
Datsun (the name was officially dropped in
1984), Infiniti (luxury model), Landcruiser
(rough-terrain vehicle, jointly built by
Toyota), Maxima, Pathfinder (rough-terrain
vehicle), Primera, Pulsar (sportscar model),
Sentra and Stanza.

NMMC   Nissan Motor Manufacturing Company USA,
             founded in 1983, in Smyrna, Tennessee.

MOSS   Market Oriented Sector Selective.

NUMMI   New United Motor Manufacturing Inc. formed in
             1984 in Fremont, California. It was a joint
             venture between Toyota Motors Corp. and
             General Motors Corp.

OEM   Original Equipment Manufacturer.

SIA   Subaru-Isuzu Automotive Inc. established in
             1989 in Lafayette, Indiana. It was a joint
             venture between Fuji Heavy Industries Ltd. and
             Isuzu Motors Ltd. See also SUBARU.

SUBARU   Japanese car line produced from 1958 to date
             by Fuji Heavy Industries Ltd. The U.S.
             representative is Subaru of America Inc.,
             headquartered in Pennsauken, New Jersey.
             Subaru became a joint venture with Isuzu Motor
             Co. Ltd. in 1989. Popular U.S. models
             include: Brat (truck model), Justy (economy
             model), and Legacy (luxury model). See also
             SIA.

TMMU   Toyota Motor Manufacturing USA Inc., formed in
             1988 in Georgetown, Kentucky.

TQC   Total Quality Control, a company-wide socio-
             technical system whose goal is constant
             improvement which is made possible by shared
             vision and goals and firms' flat, team-based
             organization structure.

TOYOTA   Japanese car line produced from 1938 to date
             by Toyota Motor Co. Ltd. The company was

established under the presidency of Risaburo Toyoda, with Kiichiro Toyoda as vice president. Its first independent vehicle factory was built in Koromo City and production began in 1938. An independent retail unit, Toyota Motor Sales Co. Ltd. was formed in 1950. Toyota Motor Sales USA Inc. was established in 1957. Popular U.S. car models include: Camry, Celica, Corolla, Corona, Cressida, 4-Runner (rough-terrain model), Landcruiser (jointly built by Nissan), Lexus (luxury model), MR-2, Starlet, Supra (sportscar model), Tercel, and Vista.

UAW   United Auto Workers union.

WA   Harmony, a managerial approach focusing on cooperation in the workplace rather than submission to authority.

Chronology

1911 Kaishinsha Automobile Factory opened its doors in Tokyo (Nissan).

1914 Kaishinsha produced its first car, the Dat.

1916 Tokyo Ishikwajima Dockland Co. Ltd. was established (Isuzu).

1917 Mitsubishi Motors Corp. was established.

1920 Toyo Cork Kogyo Co. Ltd. was founded by President Jujiro Matsudo. This marked the beginning of the Mazda Motor Corp.

1925 Ford Motor Co. formed a subsidiary in Japan. Assembly began in Yokohama.

1927 Toyo Kogyo Co. Ltd. was established.

1930 The three Japanese financiers: Den, Aoyama, and Takeuchi formed a car company called: Kai Shinsha Motors. The cars manufactured by the company took the three initials of the financiers: D.A.T. "Datson" means to promote the car as the son of the three gentlemen; since "son" means "loss" in Japanese, the result was to change it to "Datsun."

1931 Toyo Kogyo Co. Ltd. began producing three-wheeled trucks.

1933 Kai Shinsha Motors merged with Kaishinsha Motor Car Works.

1934 Datsun was renamed Nissan Motor Co. Ltd.

1937 Tokyo Ishikwajima Dockland Co. Ltd. changed its name into Tokyo Jidosha Kogyo Co. Ltd. This marked the beginning of the Isuzu Motor Co.

Toyota Motor Co. Ltd. was established under the presidency of Risaburo Toyoda with Kiichiro Toyoda as vice-president.

1938 Toyota's first independent vehicle factory was built in Koromo City and car production began.

1948 Honda Motor Co. Ltd. was founded in Hamamatsu, Japan by President Soichiro Honda.

1949 Isuzu Motor Co. Ltd. was established.

1950 Toyota's independent retail unit, Toyota Motor Sales Co. Ltd. was formed.

1957 Toyota Motor Sales USA Inc. was established. Toyota Corona was exported to the United States for the first time.

1958 Datsun, by now renamed Nissan Motor Co., entered the American auto market with Datsun 310, now named Bluebird.

1967 Mazda Motor Corp. introduced the rotary engine. It was not successful.

1968 Datsun 510, designed for the U.S. market, was introduced.

1970 Joint venture between General Motors and Isuzu was formed.

Sales of the Mazda cars began in the United States by the Mazda Motors of America Inc.

1971 Isuzu Motor Co. Ltd. became a joint venture company with General Motors Corp., with the capital participation of 34.2% by General Motors.

1973 The first Honda Civic released on the market.

1975 Nissan Motor Co., passed Volkswagen as the leading importer in the United States.

1979 Honda of America Manufacturing Inc. was built in Marysville, Ohio.

Ford Motor Co. rescued the Mazda Motor Corp., which was floundering due to the failure of its rotary engine introduced in 1967, by acquiring 25% of the Mazda Motor Corp.

1981 Datsun changed its name in the U.S. to Nissan in order to match the parent company.

1982 Honda Motor Co. Ltd. was established in Marysville, Ohio.

Toyota Motor Co. Ltd. merged with Toyota Motor Sales Co. Ltd. and changed its title into Toyota Motor Corp.

1983 Production of Nissan Motor Co. Ltd. began in Smyrna, Tennessee.

1984 New United Motor Manufacturing Inc. (NUMMI) was founded in Fremont, California. It was a joint venture between Toyota Motors Corp. and General Motors Corp.

Japan's output of automobiles totaled 11.5 million units, occupying a share of 30% in world production.

General Motors ranked first in global auto production; Toyota, the second; Ford, the third; and Nissan, the fourth.

Toyo Kogyo Co. Ltd. changed its name to Mazda Motor Corp.

1985 Nissan's U.S. car and truck sales peaked at 831,000.

1986 Ford Motor Co. opened a plant in Hermosillo, Mexico. The plant was modeled after Mazda's Hofu factory. Ford's new plant assembled the Mercury Tracer which was recognized as the company's best-built car.

1987 Mazda Motor Manufacturing USA Corp. was established in Flat Rock, Michigan. The company began by producing the Mazda MX-6 and the Ford Probe sport coupes in the U.S. It is the only Japanese plant in the U.S. to negotiate with the United Auto Workers.

1988 Diamond-Star Motors Corp., a joint venture between Mitsubishi Motors Corp. and Chrysler Corp. was founded in Normal, Illinois.

Toyota Motor Manufacturing USA Inc. was formed in Georgetown, Kentucky.

1989 Subaru-Isuzu Automotive Inc. was established in Lafayette, Indiana.

Honda Motor Co. Ltd. was formed in East Liberty, Ohio.

Nissan's Infiniti luxury cars make their debut.

1990 The Big Three took 66% of the U.S. market share.

Japan took 27.1% of the U.S. market share.

Japanese companies owned wholly or in part more than 270 auto parts suppliers in the United States. These Japanese-owned and joint-venture parts suppliers represented an employment of more than 30,000 American workers with an estimated investment of $5.5 billion in this country.

Japan's automobile industry market share reported by JAMA: Toyota Motor Corp., 32.2%; Nissan Motor Co., 18.1%; Mitsubishi Motors Corp., 9.1%; Honda Motor Co., 8.7%; and Mazda Motor Corp., 7.6%.

1991 The Big Three took 68% of the U.S. market share.

U.S. car and truck sales slumped to 584,000, lowest since 1982.

Japan's U.S. market share climbed up to 29.1%.

Nissan and Ford established a joint venture in Avon Lake, Ohio.

1992 With 75% domestic content, the new MX-6 and Probe would be the first "domestic" cars built by a Japanese plant in the U.S. The new car began production in winter 1992 by the Mazda Motor Corp.

Nissan's new sedan, known as Altima, introduced to the U.S.

Isuzu Motors Ltd. announced the plan to cease production of passenger cars in the U.S.

1993 Toyota's second U.S. plant will begin operation in Kentucky, with an estimated annual production capacity of 200,000 units.

Part I

BOOKS, DOCUMENTS, MONOGRAPHS, AND ARTICLES

1

History and Development
of the Japanese Automobile Industry

1. "All about luxury cars: a race for the young and affluent." New York Times. (September 9, 1991): F10.

   Describes the luxury car market in the United States, Japan, Europe, and West Germany. In Japan, the Honda Acura NSX and Mitsubishi Diamonte are both new entrants in addition to the Toyota Lexus and Nissan Infiniti.

2. "The Ambush awaiting Japan." Economist. 320 (July 6, 1991): 67-68.

   The Japanese automobile industry performs well even in the current economic slump which affects worldwide manufacturing industries. There are three good reasons for this: 1) Japanese lean production methods provide the most efficient way of streamlining the entire production process through the precise coordination and timing of parts, materials, and processes in the assembly room; 2) Even during business recession, the Japanese automakers outperform the market; and 3) They make cars which satisfy every personal taste and desire. Japan's automakers are facing certain obstacles in their long distance expansion abroad. Problems include the Big Three's "dumping" minivans in the American market and the U.S. investigation of Honda's overstating the North American content of vehicles it makes in Canada.

3. "America's luxury-car market: elegant Nippon." Economist. 317 (December 8, 1990): 73.

   Since Honda established its Acura division in America in 1986, Toyota's Lexus and Nissan's Infiniti lines were set up in the United States successively. Followed by the trend of promoting luxury cars in the U.S. market, Mitsubishi and Mazda launched luxury cars in America as

well.   This article gives a full account of Japanese
luxury car sales in America and analyzes the present
competitive situation among the U.S., Japanese, and
European upscale markets in the United States.

4. "American   carmakers: taking   root   and   blooming."
   Economist.   311.7598 (April 15, 1989): 79.

   Japanese transplants are quite confident of their
   automaking business in the United States.   Honda Motor
   Co., Ltd., the fourth largest carmaker in the U.S.,
   started manufacturing motorcycles in the U.S. in 1979.
   Then it began making cars from 1982.   Honda watched
   carefully what American tastes are, and designed their
   cars exclusively for the American market.   The company
   plans to export 50,000 cars a year to Japan from the
   United States by 1991.

5. Ancillary industries for automobile manufacture in Japan.
   New Delhi, India: National Productivity Council, 1966.

   This report is presented by the Study Mission on the
   Development of the Ancillary Industries for Automobile
   Manufacture in Japan.   The broad objective of the Study
   Mission is to study the productivity aspects of the
   Japanese ancillary industries for automobile manufacture
   and their relationship with the main industrial
   enterprises.   The specific areas of this study include:
   structure and growth of ancillary industries; standards
   and quality control; cost, supplies, and productivity;
   and exports.   The major focus of this report is on the
   phenomenal progress the Japanese automobile industry has
   made in less than a decade and the principal factors that
   have contributed to this achievement.

6. Aoki, Doichi.   "Strong domestic economy keeps auto
   industry rolling."   Business Japan.   34.11 (November
   1989): 51-57.

   This report describes Japanese economic conditions in
   general, and the automotive industries in particular, for
   the fiscal year 1988, and the outlook of fiscal year
   1989.   During the fiscal year 1988, domestic auto sales
   increased, export sales dropped.   However, total vehicle
   production still rose due to the strong domestic demand.
   Japan was confronted with several major tasks, such as:
   trade problems and U.S. protectionism, auto-related tax
   system changes, the impact of the unification of EC
   market, and revised standards for light cars.
   Suggestions were made by the author for the purpose of
   promoting growth and expansion of the Japanese auto
   industry.

7. Aoki, Doichi.   "The auto industry focuses on domestic
   demand."   Business Japan.   33.11 (November 1988):
   133-39.

   The Japanese auto industry still held a strong position
   in fiscal year 1987.   The domestic demand for passenger

cars was up 4.1% from the previous year and was the highest record in its history. Car exports were down 4.5% in 1987 from the previous year due to the appreciation of the yen. From the analysis shown in this article, there are two major difficulties that the Japanese auto industry has to overcome in order to continue its growth under the current business situations. First, to promote internationalization further by expanding local industries, carrying out automobile operations in many parts of the world, and providing technical aid and management techniques to the local people. Second, to make further efforts toward the expansion of domestic demand by applying product innovation, new model design, or incorporating new techniques, materials, or functions.

8. Aoki, Doichi. "Present condition and future tasks of Japan's auto industry." Business Japan. (October 1985): 57-63.

The Japanese automobile industry remained in a strong position in 1984. Export sales to the U.S. market have been quite active due to the stabilized economy. Domestic auto sales were up 1% in 1984 over the previous year. Exports were 7.8% higher for the same period. Japan's future task is related to energy-saving, atmospheric pollution control, and auto safety. The goal of seeking a higher degree of internationalization will be the mandatory task of the Japanese auto industry.

9. "Auto parts makers must cope with fall in output." Business Japan. 35.10 (October 1990): 53-56.

Due to the rapid development of Japanese passenger cars and their exports beginning around 1965, the Japanese auto parts industry prospered until its present status of maturity. Auto parts production in fiscal year 1988 increased 3.6% over the preceeding year, while exports fell 1.2%. Except raising productivity and lowering cost, auto parts makers put more emphasis on achieving better and lighter quality bodies, engines, and other equipment in order to match diversified and discriminative user needs. Light materials such as aluminum and plastics are used more often in recent years for the purpose of building auto parts with greater strength, longevity, and flexibility.

10. "Auto sector employs one in ten of Japan's workers." Business Japan. (May 1990): 31-41.

The status of the automobile industry in the entire Japanese economy is described. Examples and survey figures show that the production of the automobile industry now makes up 10% of Japan's entire manufacturing industries and 30% of its machinery industries. Issues under present discussion include: the role of the auto industry in the Japanese economy; auto equipment investment; import and export volumes; types of vehicles

under production; domestic and overseas production
activities; and foreign trade problems.

11. Behar, Richard. "Arms race on wheels." Forbes. 143.4
    (February 20, 1989): 60-64.

    Grand Prix auto racing is the world's leading racing
    program with the most advanced technology in
    sophisticated engines. It is largely dominated by the
    Honda Motor Co. of Japan. The big investment for Honda,
    while spending more than $50 million each year, is not
    simply to win the race, but to help the company to get a
    bigger share of the European auto market for the years
    ahead.

12. "Big Three auto firms move to appeal decision on sales of
    Toyota minivans." Wall Street Journal. (August 7,
    1992): B3.

    In May 1992, the U.S. Commerce Department found that
    Toyota Motor Corp. was pricing its minivans illegally at
    about 10%, or $1,500 below fair market value. The Big
    Three automakers then appealed a U.S. government decision
    that they were not being hurt by the sales of Toyota
    minivans in U.S. for less than in the Japanese market.

13. Borrus, Amy. "Not all Japanese carmakers are
    powerhouses." Business Week. (February 19, 1990):
    46-47.

    Although Japanese cars are widely known as profit-making,
    Japan's smaller auto companies are struggling to survive
    their markets. In this article, Japan's small
    automakers, Daihatsu, Isuzu (maker of Subaru cars), and
    Suzuki relate their tough experiences in auto sales and
    fierce market competition with other domestic automakers.
    Major attributes for these smaller players are: tax
    changes in Japan, loss of government protection, a
    tougher export outlook, and enormous financial demands.

14. Brooke, Lindsay. "Japanese jewels: Mazda's slick little
    1.8 L V6 could ignite a new wave of small-displacement
    engines from Japan." Chilton's Automotive Industries.
    171.9 (September 1991): 52-55.

    Mazda Motor Corp. is presenting a 1.8 L four-cam V6 in
    its MX-3, a new entry in the highly competitive sports
    car market. Mitsubishi is also considering building the
    same type of engine in its new models. Other major auto
    companies do not agree with the idea. They argue that
    the V6 engine is less cost-effective to build, and also
    less fuel-efficient, than the traditional four-cylinder
    engines. Although the wonderful motion and super
    performance the MX-3 offer give definite advantages for
    enjoying an impressive ride, most auto experts are still
    wondering whether the price is too high to pay for this
    comfort.

15. Brooke, Lindsay. "Lexus: Toyota blitzes the luxury front." Chilton's Automotive Industries. (August 1989): 40-43.

   With its LS400, the world's most efficient automaker changes the rules for building luxury-class automobiles. This article describes in detail the new design of Toyota's LS400 model. It includes an analysis of the luxury car market, the structural comparison of LS400 with "regular" cars on internal engines, speed efficiency, and oil consumption.

16. Brown, Stuart F. "The theme is green." Popular Science. 240.2 (February 1992): 50-55.

   At the recent Tokyo Motor Show, Japan's auto industry shows a major move on environmental concerns. High efficiency and low emissions are two primary focuses of modern Japanese auto-manufacturing design. Companies like Toyota, Nissan, Honda, Mazda, and Mitsubishi all expressed their environmental consciousness at this auto event.

17. Browning, Robert J. "Detroit '89: forging foreign alliances." Machine Design. 61.1 (January 12, 1989): 86-95.

   The introduction of new products in the U.S. auto market during the year of 1989 was led by joint collaboration efforts among major U.S. and Japanese manufacturers. This article describes these new product lines and their main design features and engine performances.

18. Bryant, Adam. "Faster recharge time for Nissan electric car." New York Times. (August 27, 1991): D5.

   Nissan Motor Corp. announced its new development of an electric car that can be fully recharged in 15 minutes. The so-called Nissan FEV, or Future Electric Vehicle, would be powered by a nickel-cadmium battery which requires a special high-energy power to recharge instead of a normal electrical outlet. With the tougher U.S. clean air laws in mind, electric vehicles seem to be ideal for the future generation. However, the vehicles' potential effects on environmental pollution could face another big challenge for Nissan.

19. Bylinsky, Genei. "Where Japan will strike next." Fortune. 120.7 (September 25, 1989): 42-52.

   With the massive expansion at home and abroad, Japanese companies are full of cash and a burst of high-tech products. Japanese cars now account for a nearly 30% share of the U.S. auto market, compared with the only 0.4% market share for American cars in Japan. Rival countries should be alert to the area where the Japanese will focus on the next phase of their competition.

20. Chandler, Clay. "Nissan boosts its import target for
    1993 by 50%." Wall Street Journal. (July 22, 1991):
    Sec. A, 5E.

    Nissan Motor Co., Japan's second largest manufacturer,
    revised upward by 50% its import target for the year
    ending March 31, 1993, and set the new goal at $1.1
    billion.

21. "Chasing Japan's Big Three." In The World of
    automobiles. Milwaukee, WI : Purnell Reference Books,
    1977, v. 9, pp. 1055-56.

    The history and development of Isuzu Motors Ltd. and the
    company's joint venture with General Motors in the early
    1970s are fully described in this article.

22. Clark, Kim B. and Takahiro Fujimoto. "The power of
    product integrity." Harvard Business Review. 68.6
    (November/December 1990): 107-18.

    The concept of product integrity begins with the role new
    products play in industrial competition and challenging
    with other products on performance and price. Companies
    that continuously develop successful products are
    themselves coherent and integrated. Honda Motor Co.,
    Ltd. is one of the few auto companies that makes the
    concept of product integrity the first step in their
    development process. The concept and the Honda Accord
    have been remarkably successful. The Accord has been one
    of the best-selling cars in the U.S. since 1982. In
    contrast, Mazda's putting racy, four-wheel steering in a
    conservative family car sent out a "mismatch" message to
    potential customers.

23. "Continuing success on two wheels and four." In The
    world of automobiles. Milwaukee, WI : Purnell Reference
    Books, 1977, v. 8, pp. 936-41.

    From producing motorized bikes to the world's foremost
    motorcycle manufacturer and a leading car builder, this
    article traces the development of Honda Motor Co. since
    its establishment in 1948 until the present time.
    Several motor vehicle designs through its developmental
    period are also presented.

24. Cook, James. "A tiger by the tail." Forbes. 127 (April
    13, 1981): 119-28.

    Japanese success in the automobile industry is due to its
    motivated workers' entrepreneurial skills and cooperation
    between government and business. This article starts
    with the early development of the Japanese automobile
    industry, the history of its major auto companies, and
    the relationship of U.S.-Japanese automobile industries,
    up to the year 1981 when Japan finally took the number
    one position in the international auto industry,
    outstripping the United States from the first place it
    had held for over 70 years.

25. Davis, Pedr.   "Honda   studies   Aussie   2-stroke."
    Automotive News. (November 26, 1990): 24.

    This article talks about the agreement that Honda Motor
    Co. signed with Orbital Engine Co. concerning the
    technological exchange for the right to study Orbital's
    two-stroke engine at Honda's research center near Tokyo.
    The two-stroke engine demonstrates lower energy
    consumption and produces 50% less hydrocarbon emissions
    at low load than a conventional four-stroke engine.

26. "Electronics take on larger role in auto parts industry."
    Business Japan. 34.11 (November 1989): 59-65.

    For the past several years, the Japanese auto parts
    industry grew rapidly. The nation played a major role in
    the sharp expansion of the passenger car market after
    1965. However, the surrounding environment has changed
    drastically for the past few years. There is a
    possibility of decreased production in the long run.
    Another concern is that the trade in auto parts is
    enormously imbalanced between the United States and
    Japan. Shown by the statistics of production figures in
    the Japanese auto parts industry, the electronic
    components have made steady progress in 1987 and
    afterwards due to the increasing demand for higher drive
    performance, safety, and comfort of automobiles.

27. "Electronics widely applied in auto parts industry."
    Business Japan. 35.5 (May 1990): 43-47.

    The Japanese auto parts industry plays a vital role in
    the expansion and success of the domestic auto industry.
    The rising value of yen, the intensified overseas
    production by automakers themselves, and the growing
    importation of parts from developing countries are all
    making the Japanese auto parts industry more competitive
    and tougher than thirty years ago. Japan's auto parts
    production enjoyed a steady growth rate of 6.9% in 1987.
    This was greater than the year before. Electronic
    controls achieved tremendous progress to meet strong
    demand for better travel safety, performance, and
    comfort. The use of electronic controls in power
    transmission and vehicle control devices was increased.
    The controls of fuel and ignition are more systemized and
    diversified.

28. Flynn, Michael S. The globalization of the Japanese auto
    industry. Ann Arbor, MI: Office for the Study of
    Automotive Transportation, University of Michigan
    Transportation Research Institute, 1990.

    This paper is the result of the Tenth International
    Automotive Industry Conference held by the University of
    Michigan in Ann Arbor. The paper includes the following
    major issues being discussed in the Conference: world
    auto production, the passenger car market in the United
    States and Japan, auto sales of major Japanese

manufacturers, the Japanese shift to the U.S. production, and North American auto-manufacturing.

29. "Four-wheel steering: round the bend." _Economist_. 311.7601 (May 6, 1989): 82.

The dispute over who owns the patent of four-wheel steering (4WS) has delayed the adoption of the technology for safer products. Japan's patent laws are written so that any minor changes in an invention must be patented separately, causing many lawsuits among competing auto companies. Honda first patented 4WS in 1978. Over the years all the leading Japanese carmakers such as Mazda, Nissan, Mitsubishi, and Toyota have taken the speed-conscious route to 4WS with more advanced developments.

30. "A giant from Japan." In _The World of automobiles_. Milwaukee, WI: Purnell Reference Books, 1977, v. 20, pp. 2341-49.

The history and development of the Toyota family, from its establishment of the Toyota Motor Co. Ltd. in 1937, followed by the formation of Toyota Motor Sales USA in 1957, then the introduction of its Corona series into the American market, to the company's current sales outlets all over the world, are fully covered in this article.

31. Goldstein, Carl. "Manufacturers see a future outside Japan." _Far Eastern Economic Review_. 142 (October 13, 1988): 68-69.

The current economic status of the Japanese auto industry is described. The latest results show that domestic sales shored up, while exports dropped down for the second consecutive year. The industry badly needs a more secure foundation for future growth. There are two major ways of doing that: 1) creation of strong overseas production bases, and 2) strategic alliances with foreign automakers. The joint collaborations between Mazda-Ford, and Mitsubishi-Chrysler are the two best examples among the previously mentioned plans.

32. Gross, Ken. "Infiniti and Lexus: a letter to Mercedes-Benz." _Automotive Industry_. 169 (August 1989): 30-32.

The letter is addressed to the Daimler-Benz Chief of Passenger Car Development, Dr. Ing Welfgang Peter, concerning the contending counterparts of the new Japanese luxury car series--Infiniti and Lexus.

33. Hadley, Eleanor M. "The secret of Japan's success." _Challenge_. 26 (May/June 1983): 4-11.

Industrial policy has played a significant role in postwar economic development in Japan. Since World War II, Japan has consciously sought efficient ways to restructure the nation's economy. The automobile industry was chosen to be the major target based on its potentiality of stimulating other industries, such as: glass, rubber, road-building machinery, and so forth. The cooperation between government officials and business leaders is the major driving force for Japan's postwar economic success. This article analyzes several factors which lead to Japanese success, using the automobile industry as an example to describe the country's current economic status.

34. "Highlights of Nissan's displays at 29th Tokyo Motor Show." Japan 21st. 37.1 (January 1992): 17-20.

   At the 29th Tokyo Motor Show, the many cars displayed by Nissan Motor Co. highlight the symbiosis of people, cars and nature. Nissan's exhibit featured five concept cars (Nissan TRI-X, Nissan COCOON, Nissan COCOON L, Nissan FEV, and Nissan DUAD), ten reference models, and the latest production models of environment-conscious cars. The main concerns of the company's cars are focused on such social issues as preservation of the environment, vehicle safety and recycling, driving pleasure, innovative styling, and passenger comfort.

35. Higurashi, Ryoichi and Momoko Ito. "Japanese automakers rethink efficiency v.s. profit." Tokyo Business Today. 60.3 (March 1992): 36-39.

   Selling good products at cheap prices is the traditional goal of Japanese corporate management. Despite global economic recession, Japan's auto production continues to remain at high levels. Nevertheless, the Japanese automobile industry is struggling for balance between good quality and poor profits. In fact, the ratio of net profit to sales for Toyota Motor Corp. is below the manufacturing average. The company's profitability has worsened because of increased capital investment and research and development outlays. Working under high production and low profits, Japan's leading auto manufacturers are pressured to shift their focus to the parts suppliers. Faced by the present situation, there is a need for the parts industry to extend business beyond the traditional "keiretsu" groupings, and to construct independent R&D facilities.

36. Holusha, John. "Japan's leadership among car makers facing tests abroad." New York Times. (April 1, 1983): A1, A12.

   Records the condition of Japan's auto industry in the 1980s and describes how its auto industry has earned a reputation for quality. In general, there are four major areas that have made Japanese cars higher in quality and lower in cost than those of American competitors: 1) Assembly--auto production lines are thoroughly designed for efficient flow; 2) Kanban system, or, "just-in-time" system; 3) Automation--robots replaced assembly line routines to reduce human exhaustion due to repetitive work; and 4) Workers--company promotes harmonious

relationships among workers, emphasizes job safety
measures and security. Complete details of the kanban
system, Japanese home market, and its export sales are
included in this paper.

37. "Honda motor: weak yen hurts Honda's net income in 1989."
    Business Japan. (June 1990): 16-20.

    This article reports Honda Motor Co.'s unaudited
    consolidated financial results for the fiscal third
    quarter and first nine months ending December 31, 1989.

38. "Honda president outlines plans for 1990." Business
    Japan. (April 1990): 35-37.

    Tadashi Kume, president of Honda Motor Inc., discussed
    the following in his 1990 New Year's address: sales
    results and plans on motorcycles, automobiles, power
    products, and motor sports; strategies for the 90's
    towards self-reliant operations in Japan, the United
    States, and Europe; and the production of the NS-X sports
    car since the middle of 1990.

39. Inaba, Yu. "Japanese automakers on the offensive."
    Tokyo Business Today. (May 1989): 6.

    Sales of imported cars continue to expand, growing by 36%
    in 1986, 48% in 1987, and 37% in 1988. Nearly 10% of
    passenger cars registered in Tokyo are imports. The key
    factors in the growth of car imports are the aggressive
    sales strategies of European and American automakers and
    the current healthy demand in Japan for cars in general.
    Market demand shifts to upscale cars after major tax
    changes in Japan since April 1, 1989. Under the new tax
    laws, the past 23% commodity tax has been replaced by a
    6% consumption tax so that the more expensive the car,
    the cheaper the price would be. The proposed unification
    of the European Community market creates other challenges
    for Japanese automakers.

40. "The industrial policies of the main manufacturers and
    the evolution of the industry in the world: Japanese
    manufacturers." In Transnationalization of the
    automotive industry. Raymond R. Sekaly. Ottawa, Canada:
    University of Ottawa Press, 1981, pp. [187]-231.

    Four major Japanese automotive manufacturers are
    described--Toyota, Nissan, Togyo-Kogyo (Mazda), and
    Honda. The discussions include three major points:
    Japanese-based establishments, industrial establishment
    abroad, and industrial strategies of these auto
    producers.

41. Japan: its motor industry and market. London: National
    Economic Development Office, 1971.

    Japan's motor industry has gone through remarkable
    progress between 1960s and 1970s. This report traces the
    underlying factors for its rapid expansion within this

period, with major emphasis on the industry's success in export markets. It also discusses the exports of UK motor vehicles and components in the growing Japanese market. Comprehensive statistical data are covered to summarize the major findings of this study.

42. "Japan: newcomer to the electronics field masters steep learning curve." Chilton's Automotive Industries. 169 (July 1989): S17-20.

This article describes the recent development of Japanese companies in the car electronics field. Japanese automakers are driven by strong demand for electronic devices, companies such as Toyota, Nissan, and Fuji Heavy Industries, are all following the trend to develop and improve their automobile engines. Some designed new systems, and some formed joint ventures, to enhance their market and strengthen consumer buying desire.

43. "Japan may build more U.S. plants if dollar slides." Automotive News. (July 25, 1988): 63.

Japanese automakers may build four more assembly plants in the United States if the yen reaches 80 to the dollar. They are expected to have a capacity of 2.1 million units in the United States by 1991, but if the U.S. dollar slides further, they might be able to sell 2.5 million vehicles at that time.

44. "Japan vehicle output dropped 7.1% in July from a year earlier." Wall Street Journal. (August 28, 1992): Sec. B, 7A.

The Japanese Automobile Manufacturers Association announced that Japan's production of cars, trucks, and buses dropped 7.1% in July 1992 from the year-earlier, totaling 1.2 million units. The only increase is the production of mid-sized passenger cars at 15% for the 15th consecutive month of year-on-year gains.

45. "Japan's $100-billion+ automotive parts market." East Asian Executive Reports. 14.1 (January 15, 1992): 9, 15-18.

The Japanese auto parts manufacturing industry plays a major role in the nation's economic development. However, there are certain changes which affect present market conditions. One of the most important changes is that Japan's auto sales boom is declining. Other major factors include export constraints on Japanese vehicles and growing pressures on Japan to increase parts sourcing from foreign countries. Currently, there are seven Japanese automakers which operate assembly plants in the United States. The international restructuring of the Japanese automobile industry in the United States is going to have a great impact on the American auto market, especially on corporate structure and management practices.

46. "Japan's auto makers joint the Weight Watchers." Wall Street Journal. (September 26, 1990): B12.

Due to the prospect of tougher U.S. legislation on air pollution and fuel efficiency, and the rising cost of oil prices, Japanese automakers are planning to produce lighter cars by the end of the decade. Aluminum will be the likely candidate for replacing steel in building auto bodies. The companies, such as Honda, Nissan, and Toyota are all seeking to cut the weight of new models by 20% to 40% through the next couple of years.

47. "Japan's car imports must try harder." Economist. 319 (June 22, 1991): 68-73.

After seven continuous years of growth, sales of Japanese imports were down by 4.5% in 1990. For the Japanese importers, the need to build bigger sales and servicing networks is the immediate trend, if they are to sell large number of cars in Japan. The Japanese auto producers have already entered the luxury car market and have also started reimporting cars into Japan from their overseas plants. Under the current environment of global economic recession, Japanese car imports must try harder in order to gain market shares and increase sales volumes.

48. "Japan's carmakers: the car as fashion statement." Economist. 313.7625 (October 21, 1989): 80-85.

The Japanese domestic car market is booming. The total domestic sales in the first nine months of 1989 grew by 15.3% over the same period last year. In all of 1988, it rose 13.5% over 1987's level, double the world rate. Catering to choosier customers at home forces Japanese carmakers to speed up their move to flexible production, either by building grander cars, or by improving the design of new models. The move will likely to cause more competition abroad.

49. "Japan's economy to shoot for stable growth in 1992." Tokyo Business Today. 60.1 (January 1992): 8.

Over four years of strong growth, Japan's economy is now in a stable condition, and growing steadily. There is a great impact by new automobile models being introduced to the domestic market. New engines of Honda Civic and Nissan Bluebird experienced a big sales jump in 1991. The domestic market grew in a steady phase, while sales in Japanese assembly plants operating in America fell slightly below level, due to the U.S. economic recession in 1991.

50. "Japan's supercars: the next Samurai." Economist. 313.7634 (December 23, 1989): 69-72.

Japanese carmakers are building their image into the luxury car market. Honda's first supercar, the NS-X (means "new-sports-car-experimental") is due in the U.S.

in the summer of 1990.   It is expected to be priced at
about $60,000.   Toyota is also working on a new prototype
called the 4500 GT.   In 1989, the luxury car market in
America went up about 825,000 sales. It is estimated that
the total sales will be up to 900,000 a year.   The
Japanese carmakers believe that the entry of both
Toyota's Lexus and Nissan's Infiniti will grab a large
portion of the luxury market in place of BMW and
Mercedes.

51. "Japanese automakers' U.S. offerings will go beyond the
    small car niches." Automotive News. (October 24, 1983):
    e1, e18.

    New models are announced for Japanese automakers. Toyota
    will offer front- and rear-wheel drive models for
    Corolla, a new minivan and four-wheel drive sport-utility
    vehicles.   Honda will redesign its Civic series and
    introduce the two-seat CRX.

52. "Japanese carmakers: downhill now?" Economist. 310.7589
    (February 11, 1989): 65-66.

    The Japanese auto industry is having problems in the
    foreign market.   Exports fell by more than 3% in 1988.
    This has been the third year decline since 1986.   With
    overcapacity at home and overinvestment abroad, Japanese
    car companies, such as Suzuki, Isuzu, and Mitsubishi
    Motors are talking about remedial measures like joint
    ventures and strategic alliances.   The auto market is
    reaching a saturation point.   The only relief for
    Japanese automakers is their auto replacement rate, which
    is the highest in the world.   It appears that the
    Japanese are going to deal with these serious problems by
    offering more rebates to consumers and dealers, and at
    the same time cutting their production margins as much as
    possible.

53. Jin, Takumi. "Auto industry braces for slump in domestic
    sales." Business Japan. 36.5 (May 1991): 39-43.

    In 1991, the U.S. auto market has dwindled due to the
    economic recession and the Persian Gulf War. A drastic
    change in the whole auto industry field appears to be in
    store.   Over a period of four years, the Japanese
    domestic market has expanded by about 1.5 times that in
    1986. However, domestic sales of new cars has started to
    slump since October 1990.   There are growing signs that
    the domestic market will plunge again in the coming year.

54. Johnstone, Bob.   "Sold on the looks: the wooing of
    consumers has moved from technology to design."   Far
    Eastern Economic Review. 147.8 (February 1990): 34-36.

    Faced with a saturated domestic market, Japanese
    automakers switch their attention to product design
    rather than to quality or price.   The rapid rise of
    product design is attributed to the effort made by

Japan's Ministry of International Trade and Industry (MITI). Several product design strategies adopted by Japanese electronic and auto companies are discussed.

55. Johnstone, Bob. "Reviving the two-stroke engine." Far Eastern Economic Review. 146.48 (November 30, 1989): 74.

The two-stroke engine seems to be ideal for luxury cars because of its simplicity and light weight. The engine not only uses half of the space of a conventional four-stroke engine but also consumes fuel more efficiently. Drawbacks are that it uses ten times as much oil as a four-stroke and produces a distinctive smoke. Building cars with the two-stroke engine that get rid of much of noise and vibration is Toyota's future business plan.

56. Judge, Paul C. "Nissan's flexible 'thinking' line for auto body assembly." New York Times. (August 25, 1991): 11.

Nissan Motor Co. announced plans to install a flexible manufacturing system at its plant in Smyrna, Tennessee. The system can reduce the total new-model changeover time from the original nine to twelve months to merely two or three months. Auto experts agree that the new invention has a significant advantage of producing small runs of a new model with more cost-efficiency.

57. Kamiya, Shotaro. My life with Toyota. [Japan]: Toyota Motor Sales Co., Ltd, 1976.

This book is based mainly on the personal account of Mr. Shotaro Kamiya and his personal experiences with Toyota Motor Company for the past fifty years. It contains an extensive history of Toyota and the Japanese automobile industry as well. Besides six chapters of auto history and a biography of the author, the book contains an appendix, arranged chronologically, from 1890 to 1976, including background information on socio-economic developments in Japan, on the Japanese automobile industry and Toyota, and on Mr. Kamiya's story.

58. Katayama, Hiroko. "Marketing, American-style." Forbes. 138.14 (December 29, 1986): 91-92.

Due to the growing competition of their domestic marketplace and sluggish auto sales, Toyota, Nissan, Honda, and other Japanese manufacturers try to increase the size of their sales forces by using so-called "American-style" marketing. Automakers are especially targeting young buyers, since they represent a potential buying force among domestic customers.

59. Kato, Seisi. My years with Toyota. [Tokyo]: Toyota Motor Sales Co., [1981].

This book is a personal history of Seisi Kato, a man who has spent more than half century with Toyota. He tells the history of one important part of the establishment of the automobile industry in Japan. This volume includes full descriptions of the historical development of the Toyota company from 1935 to 1980, together with its business strategies, organization, and technological innovations introduced through these years.

60. Katz, Harold. The decline of competition in the automobile industry, 1920-1940. New York, NY: Arno Press, 1970.

This book not only provides an historical background of the automotive industry from its origin to about 1920, but it also attempts to justify the extent of economics of scale for the surviving companies through those early developmental stages and how they have changed over the years. The automobile production and distribution processes are carefully examined to see what factors kept the increasing minimum sizes of the cars necessary for survival as the industry developed. All of the results are summarized by presenting an industry average cost curve, and showing how it has changed over time.

61. Keller, Maryann. "Lexus versus Infiniti: luxury battle--round two." Motor Trend. 42.12 (December 1990): 130.

After a year of launching luxury models, both Lexus and Infiniti outperformed many other long-term established luxury brands in the American auto market. The move marks a new trend for the Japanese automakers to compete with other luxury models in the upscale market. The success of Lexus LS400 and Infiniti Q45 is discussed.

62. Kindel, Stephen. "What price freedom? A changing world poses serious challenges to the future of the automobile." Financial World. 158.17 (August 22, 1989): 57-58.

Rising gas prices and consumer demands for improved safety and quality are major concerns which affect the auto business today. Even though the auto sales are beginning to slow, the demands on manufacturers are increasing. Faced with the current situation, U.S. automakers need to work even harder to challenge Japanese cars in a highly competitive way.

63. Kobe, Gerry. "Engineer for right-hand steer: how Honda does it." Chilton's Automotive Industries. 172.3 (March 1992): 34-37.

The provision of the right-hand-drive (RHD) vehicle for export to Japan has been a hot issue since President Bush's recent visit to Japan. The Big Three are now in place to develop various models of RHD vehicles. Honda's Marysville, Ohio plant researched the marketing of both LHD and RHD vehicles in the early 1990s. Through

climbing sales figures from selling of these RHD models,
the company has already started definite plans of
developing various RHD vehicles for not only the Japanese
market but also European countries. The engineering and
design of Honda's RHD models built at its Ohio plant are
fully described in this article.

64. Kuroda, Naoki. "A status report on Japan's domestic and
    foreign auto markets." Business Japan. 30 (October
    1985): 45-55.

    The following major topics are covered in this report: 1)
    status of the automobile industry in Japan's industries;
    2) management situations of Japanese automakers; 3)
    status of Japanese automakers in the world auto market;
    and 4) trends and outlooks of the Japanese auto market.

65. Landler, Mark. "No joyride for Japan: Nissan and Toyota
    are hitting bumps in the U.S. luxury car market."
    Business Week. 3141 (January 15, 1990): 20-21.

    The Japanese have been wagging a costly battle to expand
    into the U.S. luxury car market since the early 1990s.
    Overall, the market shares for Toyota's Lexus line and
    Nissan's Infiniti have been flat ever since their
    introduction into the American market. One possible
    reason is that, after years of strong auto sales, the
    whole auto market is down. To overcome this, both Nissan
    and Toyota plan to invest heavily in 1990 in an
    advertising campaign against the United States and
    European upmarket rivals.

66. Levin, Doron P. "Too American for its own good?" New
    York Times. (October 27, 1991): 1, 6.

    Among the major Japanese auto giants, Toyota is the no.
    1 vehicle producer in the United States. At a time when
    the economic recession pulled American auto sales down,
    and the market shares of combined Japanese imports and
    transplant productions only slightly affected, Toyota
    became a prime target of American reprisals. This
    article describes the trade tensions between Toyota Motor
    Sales USA and the Big Three, and reports the sales of
    Toyota's pickups concerning the Bush Administration's
    dumping investigation early this year against Japanese
    importers of minivans.

67. Levin, Doron P. "A fuel-efficient grab for power: new
    Honda spurs U.S. mileage debate." New York Times.
    (September 20, 1991): D1, D3.

    Honda Motor Co. announced its new 1992 Civic VX. The car
    is equipped with a VTEC-E engine (an acronym for Variable
    value-Timing and lift Electronic Control system-Economy),
    a highly fuel-efficient car that is expected to reach 55
    miles per gallon on the highway and 48 miles per gallon
    in the city. Detroit is concerned that the Civic VX may
    become a powerful weapon in the hands of those who favor
    stiffer auto fuel-efficiency standards.

68. Levin, Doron P. "Japan's rich cars enrich dealers." <u>New York Times</u>. (November 6, 1990): D1, D7.

    This article shows that dealerships in Japanese luxury cars are turning high profits. Those models that are most in demand include Toyota-Lexus, Nissan-Infiniti, and Honda-Acura. One example in this text describes the vigorous effort and high quality service that Lexus car dealers provided, while other American car dealers' service was far from comparable. The article suggests that Japanese auto dealers opened a new horizon in this competitive field and created this recent trend in the automobile dealers' market.

69. Lowry, A. T. <u>A financial assessment of the Japanese motor industry</u>. London: The Economist Intelligence Unit, 1988.

    Japanese motor industry has been affected by the appreciation of the yen since 1985. This has had a severe impact on the prices of Japanese products selling in world markets. Against the effective price increase due to the appreciation of the yen, the Japanese automotive industry took immediate action by stabilizing its production volume. The continued volume increase was achieved both by aggressive marketing in Japan and by increased focus on overseas sales. This report traces the financial assessment of eleven Japanese motor manufacturers, namely, Toyota, Nissan, Honda, Mitsubishi, Mazda, Suzuki, Fuji Heavy Industries, Daihatsu, Isuzu, Hino, and Nissan Diesel. It discusses the financial strategy and corporate restructuring of these companies in response to currency fluctuation.

70. "Made in Japan, sold in U.S.: how auto importers ranked in '86." <u>New York Times</u>. (January 28, 1987): 29.

    The total sales of Japanese imports in 1986 reached 2.24 million units. Separate sales figures for the Japanese auto companies are also shown in this report.

71. Maskery, Mary Ann. "Japan: automakers expected to prosper, but growth may trail 1989 because of higher costs." <u>Automotive News</u>. (January 1990): 29.

    Japan's domestic car market reports continued growth, but not as quickly as during 1989, when tax reform reduced the cost of buying large cars. There are a couple of factors that triggered the current situation. Marketing investment money spent on research for developing and designing new models, labor shortages, plant renovation and automation, and so forth, are all major factors that resulted in higher cost and lower profits in 1990. Toyota was reported to be the biggest money maker in the Japanese auto industry in 1989, while Fuji Heavy Industries was the only one that lost money.

72. "Mature markets and producers: Japan." In The future of
    the world motor industry. London: Logan Page, 1980, pp.
    [211]-46.

    The success of the Japanese motor industry's development
    has long been recognized throughout the automobile
    industry. This paper reviews the evolution and auto
    market development in Japan, including analyses of hidden
    obstacles for imports into Japan from overseas
    manufacturers, structure of the Japanese auto industry,
    share of the domestic auto producers, exports of motor
    vehicles to the U.S., Europe and Near Eastern countries,
    and the labor and productivity in Japan.

73. "Mazda eyes more North American imports in new fiscal
    year." Business Japan. 35.7 (July 1990): 18-19.

    Mazda Motor Corp. initiated an Import Expansion Action
    Program on October 1989 with the intent of increasing
    globalization of the Japanese economy and promoting
    international cooperation between nations, particularly
    in North America, in resolving trade frictions. The
    major goals of this program include: 1) promoting joint
    development with parts suppliers abroad, 2) emphasizing
    R&D in North America, 3) improving parts and components
    procurement functions and enhancing distribution
    processes in North America, 4) conducting more surveys
    for increasing Mazda's import opportunities, and 5)
    expanding imports by Mazda suppliers in Japan.

74. "Mazda markets Anfini MS-8 in Japan." Japan 21st. (June
    1992): 12-13.

    The announcement made by Mazda Motor Corp. concerning its
    introduction of the Anfini MS-8, a brand new mid-size
    four-door passenger car series in the domestic market is
    described in this article. Major features of exterior
    styling, interior design, and engine and safety concerns
    are fully described.

75. "Mazda motor: Mazda opens M2 building in Tokyo." Japan
    21st. (March 1992): 12-15.

    Recent updates of the Mazda Motor Corp. are described in
    this article. Major issues include: 1) the completion
    and opening of the M2, Inc. on December 1991 in Tokyo;
    the new company will provide vehicle research, planning,
    and design facilities for Mazda's overall product
    development system; 2) Mazda's announcement of the new
    target to promote U.S. auto industry collaboration. It
    includes increased purchasing of U.S.-made parts and
    materials, as well as of U.S.-made vehicles to be
    marketed in Japan; and 3) release of the company's
    financial results for April through September 1991.

76. "Mazda motor: Mazda introduces full-time 4WD Anfini MS-6
    in Japan." Japan 21st. (May 1992): 21-23.

Mazda Motor Corp. announced a full-time version of the
Anfini MS-6 in Japan. The car is actually the Japanese
market version of the Mazda 626. The major technical
features of the car are described.

77. "Mazda plans entry into U.S. market for luxury cars."
    Asian Wall Street Journal Weekly. (August 26, 1991): 8.

    Mazda Motor Corp. will launch a new luxury car called
    Amati in the United States in spring 1994. The intended
    sales volume and new product development plans are
    described in this report.

78. "Mazda to create second sales network in U.S." Comline
    Transportation. (August 22, 1991): 1.

    Mazda Motor Corp. announced its new plan to expand a new
    sales network for an upscale model "Amati" which will be
    on the market in early 1994. The annual sales target
    will be set at 20,000 units in the U.S. and 1,000 in
    Canada. The report points out recent developments in the
    company and describes its progress toward the luxury car
    market.

79. Meyer, Richard. "The yen for cars." Financial World.
    158.17 (August 22, 1989): 52-53.

    The Japanese auto market strategy and market shares
    information are analyzed. Current market shares of auto
    manufacturers are: Toyota: 42%, Nissan: 23%, and Honda,
    Mitsubishi, and Mazda all hover under the 10% mark. To
    meet with the domestic competition, those automakers are
    either redesigning their cars, or introducing new luxury
    models into the market in order to win big sales.

80. Miller, Karen Lowry. "Can this hot-rodder make Honda
    racing again?" Business Week. 3168 (July 9, 1990):
    58-59.

    Nobuhiko Kawamoto, the new president of the Honda Motor
    Co., is planning to set up the firm's image in sports car
    design and advanced technology. Honda's share of U.S.
    passenger car sales is 8.1% currently, while Toyota only
    has 8.5% for the same period. The only problem is the
    domestic market. Kawamoto's strategy will be to set up
    a program for decentralizing global operations in order
    to meet Honda's individual market needs.

81. Miller, Krystal. "Mazda to follow rivals in selling
    luxury marque." Wall Street Journal. (August 16, 1991):
    B1, B4.

    Followed by Lexus, Infiniti, and Acura, the luxury brands
    of Toyota, Nissan, and Honda, Mazda Motor Corp. is ready
    to enter the luxury car market. Mazda plans to introduce
    Pegasus for the 1992 model year. The car will be priced
    under $40,000 and apply a V-12 engine. Competition in
    the luxury car market has grown fiercely. However,

economic recession and the federal luxury auto tax affect the sales of high-priced vehicles as well.

82. Miyakawa, Yasuo. "The transformation of the Japanese motor vehicle industry and its role in the world: industrial restructuring and technical evolution." In Restructuring the global automobile industry: national and regional impact. Law, Christopher M., ed. London ; New York, NY: Routledge, 1991, pp. 88-113.

This article focuses on the historical and geographical development of the Japanese automobile industry, and shows how the country has involved itself in the highly competitive global market and then transformed itself into the world's leading motor vehicle producer in less than two decades.

83. "The next age for Japan's cars." Economist. 316.7664 (July 21, 1990): 63-64.

Although auto sales in Japan increased by 18.5% in 1989, the market is changing. More top-line models and bigger cars are sold due to the tax-cutting policy. Faced with the current market trend, automakers are concentrating more on redesigning new models to fit customers' tastes than mass-manufacturing the old, popular models.

84. "The nightmare scenario: Japan's motor industry." Economist. (September 19, 1992): 80-82.

The Japanese automobile industry is facing serious problems on declining sales. Every Japanese automaker, except Mitsubishi Motors, now expects a fall in profits this year. Domestic vehicle sales dropped drastically, with a rate of 15% in August, which was the lowest figure in 12 years. Auto experts attribute these problems to three major issues which Japan's car exporters once enjoyed, but now are taken over by the American manufacturers: 1) lower labor costs, 2) lower capital costs, and 3) "just-in-time" delivery. The changing pattern and transition period of each category over the past decade is clearly described in this paper.

85. "Nissan motor: lightweight transmission developed for Nissan's front-wheel-drive autos." Business Japan. (April 1990): 24-25.

Nissan Motor Co., Ltd. has developed a new-generation four-speed automatic transmission boasting the world's lightest weight for a planetary gear type automatic transaxle of its class used in front-wheel-drive cars. The major technical highlights are outlined in this article. Nissan plans to adopt this new technology in nearly all of the company's front-wheel-drive models during 1990.

86. "Nissan motor: Nissan develops 'smart' transmission." Business Japan. (September 1989): 14-15.

The description of Nissan's development of the world's first electronically controlled five-speed automatic transmission for passenger car use to be equipped with a torque converter is covered in this article.

87. "Nissan motor: Nissan Primera released on domestic market." Business Japan. (May 1990): 16-18.

Nissan Motor Co., Ltd. has released on the domestic market the Nissan Primera, a totally new medium-sized sedan. Major features of this model are outlined below: 1) exterior--new functional beauty represented in advanced styling; 2) interior--pursuit of comfort and function appealing to human sensitivities; and 3) performance highlights--supple and reassuring dynamic performance.

88. "Nissan motor: Nissan commences new international cooperation program." Japan 21st. (March 1992): 17-21.

Nissan Motor Corp. releases recent activities of the International Cooperation Program targeted on increasing imports into Japan, establishing global R&D, production, and sales systems, and enhancing industrial joint ventures with foreign firms. The company plans to increase its purchases of U.S.-made auto parts and materials with a targeted $3.3 billion in its 1994 fiscal year. Nissan's financial results for the first half of fiscal 1992 and its overseas production for the same period are also included in this report.

89. "Nissan motor: strengthened product line will boost sales, says Nissan president Kume." Business Japan. (April 1990): 19-21.

The president Yutaka Kume's speech to employees of Nissan Motor Co. is included. The article reviews the company's development in 1989 and also projects the outlook for 1990.

90. O'Neill, Brian. "Get with the program." Insurance Review. 51.5 (May 1990): 59-60.

Although Japanese cars have gained the highest reputation for quality, reliability, and cost-efficiency in the global automobile market, there is one important area where the Japanese automakers cannot take the number one position: auto safety. Many of the Japanese cars are not supplied with antilock brakes and air bags. Currently, it is the U.S. and European auto industries that are pioneering in the area of auto safety. Overall, it is time for Japan to change this image and to reconsider its marketing and manufacturing priorities.

91. Odaka, Konosuke, Keinosuke Ono and Fumihiko Adachi. The automobile industry in Japan: a study of ancillary firm development. Tokyo, Japan: Kinikuniya Co., 1988.

Describes author's interviews conducted at ten companies,
two assemblers, and eight parts suppliers, which took
place between January 1976 and August 1979. The
underlying chapters cover information in the following
areas: 1) technological development of the firms; 2)
interfirm linkages between assemblers and parts
suppliers; and 3) policy implications of these companies.

92. Ohara, Atsuko. "Toyota reports net fell 2.2% in year."
Wall Street Journal. (August 29, 1991): A7.

Toyota Motor Corp. announced its status in this report.
The company's net income is 2.2% lower than the same
period a year before, but its combined sales grew 7.2%
this year. Heavy burdens on capital investment and labor
cost, along with the strong yen hurt the company's
profit.

93. Ota, Fusae. "Competing the Japanese way." World Press
Review. 39 (March 1992): 33.

In the Japanese automobile industry, "keiretsu" refers to
the close affiliations between suppliers and
manufacturers. Japanese companies maintain long-term and
cooperative relationships with the suppliers on whom they
depend so heavily. By working closely with them,
Japanese firms can reach a production cycle of four or
five years, significantly shorter than American
automakers. The Big Three have begun modifying their
production methods along similar lines.

94. "The overseas motor industries: Japan and the new
production countries." In The motor industry : an
economic survey. London: Butterworths, 1972, pp.
188-219.

The history and development of Japanese automobile
industry from 1940 to 1970 is described. This chapter
discusses the major auto manufacturers in Japan,
including Toyota, Nissan, Daihatsu and Toyo Kogyo
(Mazda). It analyzes the traditional production
structure of these firms, the role of the Japanese
Ministry of International Trade and Industry (MITI) and
foreign trade, and the marketing and exports of Japanese
vehicles.

95. PE Consulting Group. Japan, its motor industry and
market: results of a study of the Japanese motor industry
and market. London: Motor Manufacturing Economic
Development Committee, 1971.

This book traces the key factors for Japan's rapid
expansion in automobile history between 1960s and 1970s,
with major emphasis on the industry's success in export
markets. Statistical data are included to support the
major findings of this study.

96. Pietrangelo, Joel. "2 strokes: Japan first again."
Ward's Auto World. (March 1990): 143.

Although Australia's Orbital Engine Co. is at the forefront of modern two-stroke automotive-engine development, it now appears that Japanese automakers will become the first to market this new technology. Both Fuji Heavy Industries Ltd. and Toyota Motor Corp. are expected to launch vehicles with two-stroke gasoline engines in 1993. Their new designs do not involve Orbital patents, thus it will be a completely different technological implementation of the same design.

97. Pollack, Andrew. "Succession at Toyota expected and praised." New York Times. (July 30, 1992): D5.

Mr. Tatsuro Toyoda was named the new president of Toyota Motor Corp. on July 29, 1992, succeeding his brother the current president, Shoichiro Toyoda. Future organization and objective of the company are detailed in this paper.

98. "Powerful challenger from the East." In The World of automobiles. Milwaukee, WI: Purnell Reference Books, 1977, v. 5, pp. 495-98.

The history and development of the Nissan-Datsun family and the growth of the Nissan Motor Co. in the United States since the early 1960s to the present are covered.

99. "Prosperity despite atomic devastation." In The world of automobiles. Milwaukee, WI: Purnell Reference Books, 1977, v. 11, pp. 1290-94.

The Mazda cars were originated in an undertaking established in 1920 called the Toyo Cork Kogyo Co. Ltd. in Hiroshima, Japan. Under the direction of Tujiro Matsudo, the president of the company, Mazda cars were developed through careful evaluation and comprehensive studies of the world auto market. During World War II, Mazda's Hiroshima factory was destroyed by the atomic bomb. The company's resurrection and amazing improvement should be attributed to its energetic workforce, skill, determination, and persistence of its leader and workers.

100. Rescigno, Richard. "Yen for the fast lane: Japanese auto makers step on the gas." Barron's. 70.7 (February 12, 1990): 16-20.

Even though the investment prospect is not quite favorable for the Japanese due to the rising cost of the yen, the business outlook for Honda, Toyota, and Nissan, the three largest Japanese automobile producers, is still very bright. This article describes the goals and production plans of these companies, as well as their marketing strategies and market shares. Major issues include: Toyota's long-term plan to meet nearly 50% of overseas demand with vehicles built locally; Nissan's entry into the luxury car market along with Toyota with a big increase in car sales annually; and Honda's U.S. sales increase of 1.8% in 1989.

101. Robertson, Ian. <u>Japan's motor industry en route to 2000</u>.
     London: Economist Intelligence Unit, 1988.

     This book analyzes the Japanese domestic and foreign
     markets up to the year 2000. The growing concern and
     future prospects of the Japanese motor industry are
     examined   with   the   following   major   discussions:
     acceleration of the overseas production program; finding
     low-cost auto suppliers in countries such as South Korea,
     Thailand, and Taiwan; global production or supply chain
     supported by joint ventures; and the protection of future
     earnings through a broader industrial base.   Major
     Japanese auto companies including Toyota, Nissan, Honda,
     Mazda, Mitsubishi, Suzuki, Fuji, Isuzu, and Daihatsu are
     analyzed in this report. A summary of Japanese influence
     on the global market for the following nations is
     covered: U.S., China, South Korea, Taiwan, and Thailand.
     The report concludes with an analysis of the Japanese
     domestic and foreign markets up to the year 2000.

102. "Rollback by Nissan, Honda and others: Toyota nearly
     reaches 50% of domestic auto share in Japan." <u>Business
     Japan</u>. 31.10 (October 1986): 44-45.

     In 1986, the market shares of Japanese auto companies
     were the following: 49.2% for Toyota, 22.8% for Nissan,
     11% for Honda, and 5.6% for Mazda. Companies like
     Nissan, Honda, Mazda, and many others were desperately
     trying to raise their market shares in order to keep
     Toyota's share below 50%. The secret of Toyota's
     strength was revealed in this report. The success of its
     business was attributed to the following factors:
     supplying cars exactly matched with user needs such as
     design, performance, and price, a powerful distribution
     system and nearly perfect user services. Besides, most
     Toyota dealers are independent enterprises, and they
     maintain direct contact with customers. These companies
     have decided to enhance their images on a long-term
     basis, and believe that they may grow into real rivals of
     Toyota one day.

103. Rubenstein, James M. "Japanese motor vehicle producers
     in the U.S.A.: where and why." <u>Focus</u>. 40.2 (Summer
     1990): 7-11.

     Japanese automakers have established stronghold positions
     in the U.S. marketplace through a series of global inter-
     relationships. Much of the U.S. economy now relies on
     Japanese transplants in the U.S. and their auto
     suppliers. This article analyzes Japanese plants and
     their joint ventures with the U.S., Japanese auto
     suppliers, and plant selection processes.

104. "Sales slump brings an end to auto industry's joyride."
     <u>Japan Times</u>. 32.8 (February 24, 1992): 1, 5.

     The Japanese automobile industry is in decline. Toyota
     Motor Corp. has cut operating income 61.6% in its
     passenger car market for the first half of 1991. The

drop is the worst for 18 years. Daihatsu Motor Corp.
announced that it is to cease production of two passenger
car models due to the company's financial losses caused
by poor sales and growing competition for small vehicles.
Other Japanese automakers also incurred financial losses,
lower earnings, and labor shortages at home.

105. Sanger, David E. "From Japan, new ways to sell yet more
cars." New York Times. (November 3, 1991): 4.

At the recent Tokyo Motor Show, Japanese autos focused on
a new vision of future direction with an array of
distinctive vehicles. At the same time, Detroit still
followed Henry Ford's idea of mass production of family
cars. Besides, none of the American automakers have
built a full design center in Japan. The Japanese,
however, are aggressively moving their design activities
out of Japan in order to design cars for different
regions and cultures. This article compares the
different auto-producing methods applied in both
countries. Major focus is placed on the trend of future
generations of cars. This includes electric cars, which
the Japanese have in the planning stage due to the
concern for fuel economy and a cleaner environment for
the future.

106. Sanger, David E.   "Soichiro Honda, auto innovator, is
dead at 84." New York Times. (August 6, 1991): A1, A15.

This article includes a full biographical description of
Mr. Soichiro Honda, an auto mechanic who went from
motorcycles to luxury cars. Honda Motor was the first
Japanese auto company to build factories in the United
States. In 1991, the company became the third largest
producer of passenger cars in America, replacing
Chrysler. Mr. Soichiro Honda died at 84. His
contribution to the Honda family was immeasurable.

107. Sanger, David E. "Fuel efficiency: new Japan coup?" New
York Times. (July 31, 1991): D1, D7.

Honda Motor Co. and Mitsubishi Motors Corp. are the two
leading Japanese auto manufacturers to challenge the
American automakers by redesigning the engines of their
compact cars to improve fuel efficiency. The new engines
use redesigned cylinders and computer controls to inject
more air into the engine cylinders, burning fuel faster
and more completely. Honda's new engine is called
VTEC-E, which features on the "swirl effect" in the
mixture of air and fuel that enters the engine's
cylinders. Mitsubishi's new engine is called the MVV for
Mitsubishi Vertical Vortex, using similar technologies.

108. Sasaki, Toru.   "How the Japanese accelerated new car
development." Long Range Planning. 24 (February 1991):
15-25.

The shortening of time in new car development is the
central theme of this article. It is estimated that a

typical Japanese car manufacturer takes three years to develop a new model while a U.S. manufacturer takes five years. This article further reviews the six stages involved in new car development and the technological applications of CAD/CAM methodologies to aid new product design and manufacturing processes. The product development process of three major Japanese auto manufacturers is described, they are: Toyota, Nissan, and Honda.

109. Sato, Takeshi and Shu Watanabe. "Carmakers apply the brakes." Japan Times. 32.24 (June 15-21, 1992): 17.

The Japanese automakers are readjusting their strategies to fit the decelerating market growth of the 1990s. Slow demand for autos on the worldwide basis caused the drastic declines of auto business and profits for all leading Japanese automakers except Mitsubishi Motors, which reported a 7.2% growth in net profit for the 1991 fiscal year. Nissan Motor Co. reported a 71.8% decrease in net profit from a year before. Mazda Motor Corp. plans to focus on promoting luxury cars. Honda Motor Co. is refocusing on finding growth opportunities in Southeast Asia, since the domestic demand was slow and the export restrictions in both the U.S. and Europe were tightened in recent years.

110. Schlesinger, Jacob M. "Japan car firms unveil engines lifting mileage." Wall Street Journal. (July 30, 1991): B1, B4.

The tighter U.S. fuel-economy laws prompted the Japanese automakers to design new engines, raising fuel-efficiency. Mitsubishi and Honda are the first two major automakers to claim they have made significant improvements on engines which can get as much as 20% better mileage for the same performance. The engines they are planning to use are called "lean-burn system." The Big Three and other Japanese carmakers are pursuing different approaches. They are working on two-stroke engines which can be half the weight of conventional engines that take four strokes in combustion.

111. Schreffler, Roger. "Inside the Lexus plant: new laser welding system eliminates 38 dies." Chilton's Automotive Industries. 172.8 (August 1992): 26.

A new assembly plant was opened by the Toyota Motor Co. inside its old Tahara facility to handle the LS300 series in the United States. The plant features two laser welding lines which will involve potential savings from die reduction to assembly line operations.

112. Schreffler, Roger. "The bubble bursts: Japan's auto industry faces a future of financial unknowns, controlled markets, and below average growth." Chilton's automotive Industries. 172.7 (July 1992): 30.

Describes the current financial difficulties of the
leading Japanese auto companies, including Fuji Heavy
Industries (Subaru) and Isuzu, Mazda, Daihatsu, and
Toyota. These companies are now making plans to reduce
capital expenditures and stabilize future productions.

113. Schreffler, Roger. "The engine is the key." Chilton's
     Automotive Industries. 172.4 (April 1992): 32.

     Lean-burn engine design is the current primary target of
     Mitsubishi's R&D development. The company spends nearly
     $200 million per year on lean-burn engine technology in
     lieu of the tightened emission standards set up by the
     U.S. government.

114. Serafin, Raymond. "Upscale stretching to Infiniti."
     Advertising Age. 60.32 (July 24, 1989): S8-S12.

     The introduction of Nissan's Infiniti and Toyota's Lexus
     lines posed a recent threat for the European as well as
     American luxury auto markets. This article gives a
     detailed account of the upscale market, the recent market
     trend, especially on the descriptions of Toyota-Lexus and
     Nissan-Infiniti models.

115. Shigemich, Takeshi. "Japanese auto industry faces
     serious dilemma." Japan 21st. (May 1992): 55-61.

     Japan's automotive industry is facing a current crisis
     for both domestic and foreign markets. Shipments of
     automobiles to the domestic market in 1991 fell 3.3% from
     the previous year. Exports in 1991 also fell 1.4% from
     the previous year. Overseas production grew by about 19%
     during the same period. Auto trade friction between
     Japan and America has been intensified since President
     Bush's visit to Japan in January. The United States put
     pressure on Japan to increase the imports of American
     made cars and parts and forced the Japanese automakers to
     increase the import of U.S. auto parts to $19,000 million
     by 1994 and sell a minimum of 20,000 American cars per
     year. Automakers have started to rebound themselves,
     including longer cycles for model changes, the reduction
     of car types, and by increasing retail prices.

116. Sinclair, Stuart W. The Japanese car industry: where now
     in the 1980s?. London: Economist Intelligence Unit,
     1984.

     This Economist Intelligence Unit Special Report examines
     the current and future issue of the structure and
     development of the Japanese car industry. It is divided
     into eleven chapters. The first four chapters cover: 1)
     the current issues facing Japanese carmakers; 2) the
     growth of the Japanese car industry; 3) a review of the
     nine companies: Toyota, Nissan, Honda, Mitsubishi, Toyo
     Kogyo, Isuzu, Fuji, Suzuki and Daihatsu; and 4) the
     production process in Japan which leads to its business
     success. The rest of the chapters analyze Japanese
     future prospects in the car industry, including the

issues of strategic options, overseas investment, process
innovation, and product strategies.

117. Solo, Sally. "Japan's new cars: they're large, powerful,
more rounded and stylish, and packed with electronic
goodies." Fortune. (December 4, 1989): 82-85.

Several new models at the Tokyo Motor Show of 1989
included features such as the hydraulic active suspension
system implemented on Nissan's Infiniti; the two-stroke
engines highlighting fuel-saving which General Motors and
Ford have licensed with Orbital, the inventor of this new
system; the traction control used on rainy, snowy, or icy
roads so that the sensors on those cars will detect wild
spinning, and automatically slow down the wheels; a
standard system used on Toyota's Lexus, Crown, and Mark
II, and U.S. Cadillac Allante.

118. Stokes, Henry Scott. "Toyota pulls away from Nissan."
Fortune. 108 (September 19, 1983): 88-95.

The competition between Toyota and Nissan in the world
marketplace is analyzed. Toyota's conservative way has
governed every aspect of its operations. While for
Nissan, with its aggressive strategies toward
technological advancement and overseas expansion, is
ahead of Toyota and remains strong. Toyota's decision on
the merger of its two principal arms, Toyota Motor and
Toyota Motor Sales in 1982 bring to the company a higher
production volume and big combined sales. Recently,
these two companies competed furiously both at home and
abroad for market share. Toyota's global sales have been
ahead of Nissan's during recent years. Although both
companies tried to re-establish their images through
internal character change, the differences between the
two go far beyond matters of style and appearance.

119. "Strong performance in first half of fiscal '90 boosts
Mazda's planning." Business Japan. 35.7 (July 1990):
15-17.

Mazda Motor Corp. reviewed its favorable performance for
the first half of fiscal 1990. The strong domestic
demand was supported by the introduction of new products,
the promotion of auto sales, and a new tax system. There
are two newly established sales channels, V and Autozama.
The former specializes in upscale European-style models,
while the latter primarily deals with micro to mini
vehicles. Exports have slightly declined as the result
of growing overseas local production.

120. Structure of the Japanese auto parts industry. Tokyo,
Japan: Dodwell Marketing Consultants, [1990].

Analyzes the infrastructure of the Japanese auto parts
industry when compared with the American auto market and
describes the operations of leading Japanese auto
companies, including the analyses of future perspectives
of these companies.

121. Tanaka, Masato. "Auto parts makers see positive increase
      in production." Business Japan. 36.10 (October 1991):
      57-61.

      In Japan, the ratio of parts production by the auto
      manufacturers themselves is quite low, it accounts for
      only 20% to 30%, while in the United States, the ratio
      is estimated about 70% to 80%. The low rate indicates
      the close cooperation of Japanese automakers with parts
      suppliers. The market in the Japanese auto parts
      industry is very competitive. Constant efforts for
      maintaining product quality and meeting demands are
      essential to win market shares in Japan. Auto parts
      production is developed along with the high growth of
      auto production in recent years. Production in 1989
      increased 23.5% over the year before. Although the rate
      slowed down at one point due to the sharp appreciation of
      the yen, production growth has steadily increased, and
      the rise in production should be expected.

122. Taylor, Alex III. "Getting a first look at Japan's new
      cars." Fortune. 124.13 (December 2, 1991): 113-20.

      The latest Japanese automotive technology was exhibited
      at the Tokyo Motor Show. This year's major design
      features focus on producing sensible, environmentally
      conscious cars. 181 new car models were shown. The
      Japanese automakers are expected to launch 120 new kinds
      of automobiles within the next five years. The trend of
      new car design will concentrate on upscale models, with
      excellent design standards and high fuel-efficiency.

123. Taylor, Alex III. "Here come the hot new luxury cars."
      Fortune. 122 (July 2, 1990): 58-65.

      Honda's four-year-old Acura division is en route to sell
      nearly as many automobiles in the $20,000 range as BMW.
      Together with Toyota's Lexus and Nissan's Infiniti, they
      should outsell BMW and Mercedes-Benz combined.
      Furthermore, within the next two years, Japan will
      introduce at least nine new high-priced models in the
      United States, including an Acura Legend that is larger
      inside than a Cadillac. The Japanese have succeeded by
      pioneering a new route to wealthy car buyers that
      combines exceptional product quality, reliability, and
      value with superior sales and service. To compete,
      European and American luxury automakers have begun using
      price as a sales weapon, which violates every principle
      of luxury marketing.

124. Taylor, Alex III. "Here come Japan's new luxury cars."
      Fortune. 120.4 (August 14, 1989): 62-66.

      The introduction of Toyota's Lexus LS 400 to the American
      auto market represents the first in a series of Japanese
      super luxury cars aimed at U.S. buyers. Nissan is
      immediately following by introducing its first luxury
      model, Infiniti Q45, and Mazda and Mitsubishi are also
      planning expensive new sedans. Toyota officials are

worried about how successful the sales are going to be
since the company has been investing heavily in this new
model with plenty of time as well as money.

125. Tomisawa, Konomi. "The auto parts industry of Japan:
facing the challenge of internationalization and
technical innovation." LTCB Research: Quarterly Review
of Japanese Industry. 74 (July/August 1984): 1-13.

Pros and cons of overseas operations and auto parts
companies' activities in the United States are described.
Statistics and projections of Japanese auto parts
industry in the U.S. are provided for the years between
1960 to 1990.

126. Toy, Stewart. "This isn't the Legend Acura dealers had
in mind." Business Week. 3081 (November 28, 1988):
106-10.

The most recent trend of the Japanese auto companies is
aiming at upscale models on the American market. Honda
Motor Co. first launched the Acura model and set up a
separate dealer network to sell it. Toyota, Nissan, and
General Motors are all trying to organize an exclusive
dealer system to market their new cars. This paper
reviews the recent market strategies of these auto
companies by detailing the marketing and sales of Honda's
Acura-Legend.

127. Toyoda, Eiji.   Toyota, fifty years in motion: an
autobiography.   Tokyo ; New York, NY: Kodansha
International, 1987.

Toyota Motor Co., the largest automobile manufacturer in
Japan, and also ranked the third as the world's global
vehicle producer after General Motors and Ford, is fully
described in this book. Mr. Eiji Toyoda analyzes the
successful history of the company, the overall profile of
Toyota's sales volume, and the reason why they reached
the number one rank in the Japanese auto industry.

128. Toyota: a history of the first 50 years. Toyota City,
Japan: Toyota Motor Corp., 1988.

TMC, the world famous Toyota Motor Co., was founded in
1937. In 1987, it celebrated its 50th anniversary. This
book, based on Toyota's fifty-year history, describes
clearly from the beginning the company's earlier years of
struggle, toward the refinement and establishment of the
whole nation's consent on high quality, super industrial
management skills, and production control, then, the new
expansion of overseas markets and joint ventures on
worldwide bases. The book is finely illustrated with all
car models the company designed through the years, maps
of overseas plants, charts and tables of the production
volumes and chronological tables of the company's
operational history.

129. Toyota: the first twenty years in the U.S.A.. Torrence,
     CA: Toyota Motor Sales, 1977.

     Established in 1957, Toyota celebrated its 20th
     anniversary on October 31, 1977. The company became the
     leading imported passenger carmaker in 1975, surpassing
     Volkswagen. Its auto sales network now spans the globe.
     This book reviews the origins of Toyota in Japan,
     describes the characteristics of its parent company, and
     traces the reasons for its incredible success. It then
     examines Toyota's foundation in the United States,
     including the company's obstacles, temporary setbacks, to
     the number one import position in passenger car sales.

130. "Toyota establishes companies in Kyushu, Hokkiado."
     Business Japan. 36.5 (May 1991): 19.

     Toyota Motor Corp. recently announced the establishment
     of two new companies in Kyushu and Hokkaido. Toyota
     Motor Kyushu Inc. will start production of passenger cars
     in early 1993. Toyota Motor Hokkaido Inc. will produce
     auto parts in the fall of 1992.

131. "Toyota motor: New Year's message boasts of Toyota's
     social and cultural efforts." Business Japan. (April
     1990): 25-26.

     Toyota Motor Corp.'s President, Mr. Shoichiro Toyoda
     delivered the New Year's message to the company's
     workforce. It outlined the business activities of the
     past year, as well as future goals and expectations for
     the year 1990.

132. "Toyota motor: overseas production doubles for Toyota in
     fiscal 1990." Business Japan. (June 1990): 13-14.

     This is a financial report of Toyota Motor's production
     in fiscal year 1990. It includes a detailed description
     of sales and production volumes, the sales breakdown for
     domestic and overseas autos, as well as the itemized
     operating income for both profits and losses.

133. "Toyota motor: popular Toyota models get minor changes
     for '89." Business Japan. 34.8 (August 1989): 16-20.

     The report of minor changes for Toyota's Corolla and
     Sprinter Series and full model change for Hilux Surf are
     described. Toyota Motor Corp.'s total production volume
     was down slightly for April 1989. However, overseas
     production was up 71.1% from that of April 1988. Total
     domestic registrations and exports in April 1989 were up,
     with the rate of 13.2% and 2.2% each over April 1988.

134. "Toyota motor: Toyota announces international cooperation
     program." Japan 21st. (March 1992): 15-17.

     The recent updates of the Toyota Motor Corp. include its
     International Cooperation Program aimed at increasing
     imports, local purchasing through its operations abroad,

and cooperation with foreign automakers; its annual organizational changes to improve the company's management and administrative structures and to enhance the corporate structure and decision-making process.

135. "Toyota Motor: Toyota presents two new minivans." Japan 21st. (April 1992): 18-20.

Toyota Motor Corp. presents two new midship-engine minivans--Estima Lucida and Estima Emina to the market. The detailed specifications of styling, power train, body and chassis, cabin space and equipment, and safety and environmental concerns of these two new series are described in this article.

136. "Toyota projects strong domestic sales in Fiscal '89." Business Japan. 34.1 (January 1989): 22-24.

This article details the Toyota Motor Corp.'s financial settlement for the fiscal year 1988. Total vehicle production in fiscal year 1988 was 3,85413,692 units. Passenger car production rose by 9.9%, but truck and bus production fell by 0.6% compared to fiscal year 1987. Total exports dropped 0.2%. Export sales remained competitive as a result of the strong yen and protectionism in both Europe and the United States. Domestic sales had steady increases over the past few years, and Toyota projected that sales for fiscal year 1989 should still remain strong.

137. "Toyota records all time high production rate in February." Business Japan. 35 (July 1990): 21-25.

The announcement of Toyota's production, domestic registration, export, and overseas production results for February 1990 are covered. Compared with the February 1989 figure, Japanese total production had a 9.4% increase, total domestic registrations were up 31.3%, and total exports were down 14.9%, separately, from last February.

138. "Trends in Japan's auto parts industry." Japan 21st. (May 1992): 63-68.

Japan's auto parts industry in 1990 enjoyed a business boom. But both domestic sales and exports began to fall in 1991. Intensified global competition and the growing financial challenge for expanding overseas markets are two major factors. Beyond that, the current trend of switching markets focused into setting up safety measures, solutions to environmental and pollution problems, as well as the development of new products have become primary duties for the auto parts industry. The recent trend of Japan's auto parts industry is summarized in this article, including the latest projections of the auto parts production, exports and imports, as well as its future investment outlook.

139. Tsutsui, Mikio.   "Japanese automakers face safety demands."   Tokyo Business Today.   59.5 (May 1991): 50-52.

Japanese cars are generally considered as better quality, reasonably priced, and fuel efficient.   However, the safety measure is always the weakest point facing the Japanese automakers.   A sharp surge in concern about automotive safety is the latest trend in the automobile industry.   Faced with this mounting movement, the Japanese government is now taking action to insure safety items to be made standard or at least optional equipment by 1993 for all domestic automakers.   Companies like Honda, Toyota, Mitsubishi, and Nissan are all prepared to meet the safety requirement set up by the Japanese government, by the target date of 1993.

140. Ueno, Hiroya and Hiromichi Muto.   "The automobile industry of Japan."   In Industry and business in Japan. Hazuo Sato, ed.   White Plains, NY : M.E. Sharpe, 1980, pp. 139-90.

The chapter starts with a description of the historical background of the Japanese automobile industry, analyzes several factors which stimulate its auto-industrial propagation, describes the Ministry of International Trade and Industry's (MITI) protection policy, and finally discusses the unique Japanese marketing and managerial techniques it applied.

141. "Used cars in Japan: young bangers."   Economist. 321.7738 (December 21, 1991): 85-87.

The Japanese motor industry is facing a serious problem: the overabundance of used cars.   Japan used to export almost 60% of the cars they produced.   But by 1990, the export proportion has slumped to only 45%.   All that excess capacity was directed to the domestic market.   The annual decline in auto sales since 1980 is also a contributing factor.   Parking and auto-traffic in Japan are part of the reasons for people not to choose driving and using public transportation instead.   This article describes the current status of the Japanese motor vehicle industry and analyzes the present problems they face as a result of the above-mentioned issues.

142. Washington, Frank.   "Japan circles the wagons." Newsweek.   116.26 (December 24, 1990): 44.

Honda Motor Co. has unveiled a family-sized wagon of its popular Accord model.   The new move places competitive pressure on Detroit's family-car market.

143. Way, Arthur.   "Hard drive from the East."   Economist. 309.7572 (October 15, 1988): S7-S8.

Japanese cars have dominated the American auto market for over a decade.   They now account for nearly 25% of the American market.   There are many reasons to explain this:

1) consistently improved productivity, 2) dedicated
workforce, 3) sensitivity to product quality, and 4)
responses to market changes and consumer needs.   In
recent years, Japanese automakers continue to shift their
production base overseas, especially America.   This
article reviews the structure and development of the
Japanese automobile industry, primarily its overseas
production in America within the past few years.

144. Womack, James P., Daniel T. Jones and Daniel Roos. The
     machine that changed the world. New York, NY: Macmillan,
     1990.

     This book is the result of a five-year study conducted by
     the research team of International Motor Vehicle Program
     (IMVP) at the Massachusetts Institute of Technology.
     Several hundred personal interviews with worldwide
     companies, governments, and unions formed the bases of
     this book. This international survey explores the major
     differences between mass production and lean production
     in the automobile industry. The theory and techniques of
     the Japanese "lean production" are analyzed. Over half
     of the world auto companies were visited and studied by
     the IMVP team in order to define the "lean production"
     system and analyze the system's impact on company's
     production control, products quality, design variations,
     and managerial strategies. The book concludes with the
     successful utilization of the lean production system
     initiated by the Japanese auto industry as a model for
     world auto companies.

145. Woodruff, David. "Japan thinks there's room for vroom in
     the U.S." Business Week. (February 27, 1989): 42.

     The recent Japanese auto-selling campaign in the United
     States is focusing on young buyers with sales of sports
     and "sporty-like" cars. Honda's NS-X, Mazda's Miata, and
     Nissan's 300 ZX are all modern product lines aimed at the
     younger American generation. Whether these sports cars
     would make a profit in the U.S. market or not is a
     critical question, especially during the economic
     downturn of the 1990s, plus higher auto insurance rates
     and very limited utility for these cars.

146. Yamaguchi, Jack K. "Japan: technology on full boost."
     In World cars. Pelham, NY : Herald Books, 1984, pp.
     62-68.

     The technological innovations on Japanese motor vehicles,
     economic conditions in the domestic auto market,
     financial status and outlook of the Japanese auto
     companies, as well as current auto model designs are all
     major areas of study in this article.

147. Yamazaki, Kiyoshi. "The internationalization of Japanese
     manufacturing firms." In Development of mass marketing:
     the automobile and retailing industries. Akio Okochi and
     Koichi Shimokawa. Tokyo: University of Tokyo Press,
     1981, pp. 215-29.

The internationalization process of the Japanese industry is explored, with major emphasis on the recent development of the Japanese automobile industry. The author makes several points for the competitiveness of the Japanese industry, such as: industrial innovation, technological difference between Japan and the United States, and the Japanese advantage of low-cost labor. Beyond that, Toyota's production system, its technological and managerial techniques are analyzed. Finally, this paper analyzes the trend of global automobile markets and compares the U.S. and Japanese automobile industries.

148. Yoshioka, Shigehira. "An overview of Japan's automobile industry." Business Japan. 36.10 (October 1991): 43-55.

In 1990, Japan's auto production accounted for 28% of the world's output. Total production in the three major auto manufacturing areas of Japan, the United States, and the European Community is reported at 79% of national output. In recent years, Japan's automobile industry has focused on the problems of auto safety, gas emissions and environmental pollution, reflecting the demands of society. The outlook for the auto industry in 1991 is for a slight gain on the domestic market over last year. Exports are expected to fall as a result of the shift of the supply source from Japanese exports to local production in North America.

149. Yoshioka, Shigehira. "The automotive industry: key to Japan's economy." Business Japan. 35.10 (October 1990): 41-51.

The current situation of the Japanese domestic and foreign auto markets are discussed. The domestic market grew rapidly from 1987 to 1990. However, export sales dwindled due to the overseas shift of their production base by Japanese automakers. The current tasks and problems of the Japanese automotive industry can be reduced to the following points: 1) the demand for the protection of the global environment, especially the legal control of exhaust fumes from automobiles; 2) traffic casualties and safety measures; and 3) response to trade and economic friction with the United States and the European Community.

2

Relationship of U.S.
and Japanese Auto Industries

150. Arnesen, Peter J., ed. <u>Is there enough business to go around: overcapacity in the auto industry</u>. Ann Arbor, MI: Center for Japanese Studies, The University of Michigan, 1988.

The main discussion of this book is the overcapacity problem in the automotive industry. Topics include: manufacturing strategy in global capacity, auto workers in a world of overcapacity, competition in the European automobile industry, and troubled sector of the parts and component suppliers' industry.

151. Arnesen, Peter J. <u>The Japanese competition: phase 2</u>. Ann Arbor, MI: Center for Japanese Studies, The University of Michigan, 1987.

This book includes lectures from the sixth U.S.-Japan Automotive Industry Conference held in Ann Arbor, Michigan. The goal of the Conference is to foster an informed response to the challenges facing the automotive industry. Issues under discussion in part I include: Japanese quality products through teamwork, the labor market, and management strategies; joint ventures as a strategy for competition; and the U.S. auto industry and world trade. Part II comprises two papers: the first paper offers a number of useful insights into the motivations of Japanese automotive assemblers, the second paper discusses the tense trade relations between Japan and the United States.

152. <u>Automotive parts industry and the U.S. aftermarket for Japanese cars and light trucks</u>. Washington, DC: Automotive Affairs and Consumer Goods, International Trade Administration, U.S. Dept. of Commerce, [1985].

This report was prepared by the U.S. Department of
Commerce, focusing on the critical sector of the
automotive industry. It is divided into two parts. Part
one presents an overview and structure of the total
automotive parts industry and analyzes its market
segments, labor productivity, regional distribution, and
trade performance over the past ten years. Part two
details one important sector of the industry: the U.S.
aftermarket (replacement parts) for Japanese cars and
light trucks. It includes a detailed description of the
competitive market challenges facing U.S. auto parts
manufacturers and identifies the U.S. trade barriers to
supplying this market and develops recommendations for
measures to be taken by the U.S. auto parts industry and
the U.S. Government to improve and support industrial
efforts in this area.

153. Bagot, Brian. "Sport/utility vehicles: urban cowboys."
     Marketing & Media Decisions. 24.8 (August 1989): 109-21.

     The top sport-utility vehicles of the U.S. market for the
     year 1988 is reviewed. Those favorite vehicles are:
     Chevrolet S-10 Blazer, Jeep Cherokee, Ford Bronco II,
     Suzuki Samurai, Isuzu Trooper II, Nissan Pathfinder,
     Toyota 4 Runner, Jeep Wrangler, and Mitsubishi Montero.
     It is estimated that upscale, active life-style oriented
     couples, aged 25-49 dominate more than 60% of the
     sport-utility vehicles market. Recognizing this trend
     will help carmakers to accelerate sales by offering more
     enhanced features for the customers' tastes.

154. Bhaskar, Krish. The future of the world motor industry.
     New York, NY: Nichols Publishing Co., 1980.

     An in-depth analysis of the world motor industry is
     covered in this book. There are four major parts in this
     book. Part one describes the current state of the
     industry, identifies the nature, shifts in production and
     demand, and socio-economic concerns for the whole
     automotive industry. In part two, three major auto
     markets and producers are analyzed, including North
     America, Western Europe and Japan. The minor markets and
     producers in South America, the Middle East, South
     Africa, Australia, and New Zealand are included in part
     three. The structure and development of the Japanese
     auto industry are discussed. The issues include
     industrial evolution, market potentials, import
     penetration strategies, competitive strengths of its
     manufacturers, and future economic prosperity.

155. Bloomfield, Gerald T. "The world automotive industry in
     transition." In Restructuring the global automobile
     industry : national and regional impact. Christopher M.
     Law, ed. London; New York, NY: Routledge, 1991, pp.
     [19]-60.

     The world automotive industry underwent a substantial
     change during the mid-1970s after the international oil
     crisis began to affect the global economy in 1973. As a

result of persistent expansion, the Japanese motor
vehicle industry replaced the U.S. as the world's leading
auto producer after 1980. This article analyzes in
detail the transition of the world automotive industry,
especially for the period after 1973, and until 1990.
The three production regions in North America (includes
the United States and Canada), Western Europe, and Japan
are discussed, with major emphasis on the Japanese motor
industry. Three case studies concerning corporate
responses to the pressures of international competition
are presented. These selected corporations represent
very different multinational business structures. They
are General Motors, Volkswagen, and Toyota.

156. Bloomfield, Gerald T. The world automotive industry.
London: David & Charles, 1978.

The first half of the book discusses the global auto
industry in general, with special discussion on the
historical development processes, innovation and
production techniques, marketing strategies, the cost
structure and management styles, location selection with
effects on motor vehicle production, and peripheral
industries. The second half describes the major auto
production bases of nine geographic areas in more than
twenty countries in the world. Chapter nine contains a
detailed analysis of the Japanese automobile industry
from its development in the 1960s to the mass-expansion
period of 1970s.

157. Boyer, Edward. "Are Japanese managers biased against
Americans?" Fortune. 114 (September 1, 1986): 72-75.

When Japanese automakers started to build plants in the
United States, domestic companies hoped to sell them a
large amount of parts. However, after these plants
successfully set up operations in this country, they also
brought along their own suppliers. Relationships between
the two are generally characterized by trust, loyalty,
and mutual respect. American suppliers are commonly
being criticized by those Japanese automakers on issues
such as quality control and cost efficiency. This paper
analyzes the inter-relationships between the Japanese and
American manufacturers and their respective suppliers.

158. Bradley, Peter. "The 1991 fleet: a model for every
need." Purchasing. 109.5 (October 11, 1990): 68-80.

Based on the review of new car products offered in 1991,
the latest developments of auto market are concentrated
in the following areas: 1) safety--the use of antilock
brakes and driver's side air bags; 2) expansion of
minivans and sport-utility vehicles; 3) the use of
computer chips to control automatic transmission and fuel
injection; 4) aggressive marketing plans on sport-utility
vehicles; and 5) provision of more flexible options to
customers. The article also covers the selective product
changes for the 1991 model year. It describes cars,

pickups, vans and minivans, and sport-utility vehicles with their redesigned features and options.

159. Browning, Robert J. "Detroit '90 motor-city slowdown?" Machine Design. 62.1 (January 11, 1990): 72-91.

This article describes the upgrades and new design features of both U.S. and Japanese cars in the 1990s. The U.S. manufacturers are focusing on mid-size and luxury automobiles. For the Japanese, new designs on popular models sold in the United States will be their major goal.

160. Bryant, Adam. "A race for the young and affluent." New York Times. (September 8, 1991): 10.

Competition in the luxury car market is getting tougher. Domestic sales fell 9% in 1990. General Motors' Cadillac division has redesigned its 1992 Seville and Eldorado for younger buyers. Meanwhile, the Japanese are keeping up with the affluent market trend. Honda's Acura division, Toyota's Lexus, Nissan's Infiniti, and Mitsubishi's Diamonte divisions are all new entrants in the luxury-car competition.

161. Bryant, Adam. "Vehicle sales fell in August." New York Times. (September 6, 1991): D1, D2.

Sales of American-made vehicles fell 11.6% in late August 1991 from a year earlier. Sales by Japanese automakers, including vehicles built in the United States, fell 5.4% for the same period. Auto experts predict that the economic downturn could keep buyers away from showrooms for a while.

162. Chang, C. S. The Japanese auto industry and the U.S. market. New York: Praeger, 1981.

This book analyzes the Japanese motor vehicle industry from the management point of view with two major aspects: its history and its impact on the U.S. market. Both external and internal forces affect the management of Japanese motor vehicle companies and the industry as a whole. The first part covers details on the historical background of the Japanese automobile industry, the internal government policies which affect its auto industry and the external environmental forces and automobile manufacturers that influence the whole Japanese auto market. The second part includes a comparative study of Japanese managerial skills versus U.S. government strategies as well as the impact of the Japanese auto market on the U.S. motor vehicle industry. Finally, an analysis of future competition and cooperation between Japan and the United States is presented.

163. Coats, Norman. "The globalization of the motor vehicle manufacturing industry." Planning Review. 17.1 (January/February 1989): 34-39.

This article presents a detailed comparative analysis of
U.S. and Japanese corporate strategies, and describes the
critical   success   factors   of   the   global   corporate
strategic trends using Japan as an example. According to
the figures compiled by the author, Japan's share of
world production on passenger cars increased from 1.27%
in 1960 to 23.8% in 1987, while the U.S. auto industry in
the same period fell from 51% to 21.4%. Thus, Japan's
auto industry has overtaken the United States in global
production since 1980. The major strategic issues in the
automotive industry fall into five categories: 1) new
technology, 2) productivity growth, 3) cost advantages,
4) corporate linkages, and 5) maintenance and growth.
Through a process of linkages and joint ventures, many
auto companies are competing reasonably well in the
marketplace.

164. Cole, Robert E., ed. The Japanese automotive industry :
      model and challenge for the future?   Ann Arbor, MI:
      Center for Japanese Studies, The University of Michigan,
      1981.

      This is the first annual conference report of the Center
      for Japanese Studies which was held in the University of
      Michigan in 1981. Many important industrial issues were
      brought up for discussion which include: U.S.-Japan
      trade relations; the future of the U.S. auto industry,
      and the Japanese challenge; government policy, business,
      and labor perspectives for both countries; Japanese
      industrial policy, its automobile management, quality
      control, and the source of strength; the comparative
      study between these two countries on quality control
      practices, labor market, management, and automotive
      technology.

165. Cole, Robert E., ed.   Automobiles and the future:
      competition, cooperation, and challenge. Ann Arbor, MI:
      Center for Japanese Studies, The University of Michigan,
      1983.

      This book includes collected papers of the 1983
      U.S.-Japan Auto Conference held in Ann Arbor, Michigan.
      Important   issues   under   discussion   include   the
      international   competition   and   auto   trade,
      internationalization of the Japanese auto industry, the
      prospects and consequences of American-Japanese company
      cooperation, opportunities and barriers to union and
      workers, the comparison of U.S.-Japan production costs,
      and the prospects and pitfalls of the future auto trade
      industry.

166. Cole, Robert E. and Taizo Yakushiji. The American and
      Japanese auto industries in transition: report of the
      Joint U.S.-Japan Automotive Study. Ann Arbor, MI: Center
      for Japanese Studies, The University of Michigan, 1984.

      During the early 1980s, the weakness of world economy and
      business   recession   accelerated   the   trade   imbalances
      between Japan and the United States. At that time, a

number of U.S. and Japanese staff in the University of
Michigan initiated a set of private discussions that led
to a formal establishment of the Joint U.S.-Japan
Automotive Study. This report is the result of the
discussions among its Policy Board members. Major
coverage of the report includes: postwar evolution of the
Japanese and American auto industries; worldwide
coordination and integration between these two countries;
macroeconomic issues and bilateral trade relations; human
resource development and labor relations; and overall
comparison and analysis of products, costs, and
technology between these two nations.

167. Cole, Robert E. "U.S. quality improvement in the auto
industry: close but no cigar." California Management
Review. 32.4 (Summer 1990): 71-85.

The question of "how to improve the quality of U.S.
automotive products in order to compete with the Japanese
auto market established in the U.S." is the central
discussion in this paper. There are several key points
brought up by the author: total quality control, customer
service and expectations, management behavior, defects
detection, performance and features of end products, and
the redesign cycles. Several charts and figures are
presented to demonstrate Japanese quality ratings, annual
production, and quality performance in the automobile
industry.

168. "Competition in the world auto industry." In Product
development performance: strategy, organization, and
management in the world auto industry. Boston, MA:
Harvard Business School Press, 1991, pp. 35-66.

This chapter analyzes the basic market structure and
regional differences among auto producers in Japan, the
United States, and Europe; describes automobile
competition in the three regions mentioned above; and
compares the strategic variations and product
performances of the Japanese, American, and European
cars. The chapter concludes with an analysis of global
auto competition and future trend of automobile
development.

169. Cordtz, Dan. "Car wars: a global report on the auto
industry." Financial World. 158.17 (August 22, 1989):
31-47.

The main topics of this report include: the market trend
of world automobile industry, the comparative analyses of
the U.S., Japanese, and European auto markets, and the
statistical analyses of international auto production,
sales volume, and market shares. Of the three major auto
markets, namely, the U.S., Japanese, and European, it is
the U.S. that today finds itself in the worst situation.
The U.S. plants depend almost entirely on the domestic
market. During the most recent years, the foreigners'
share of the U.S. sales have continued to grow and the
Japanese accounted for a total share of nearly 40% of the

U.S. auto market. This growing pattern is a major threat
for the Big Three. Detroit tries to catch up by
emphasizing quality, performance, and new design
features.

170. "Detroit beware: Japan is ready to sell luxury."
     Business Week. 2927 (December 9, 1985): 14, 18.

     The U.S. auto industry is threatened by the new trend of
     Japanese luxury car imports. Auto analysts predict that
     foreign carmakers will move to 2.8 million cars in the
     United States in 1985, and will reach 3 million in 1986.
     The shift of the Japanese car market to luxury models
     hurts Detroit which has been relying heavily on luxury
     cars for profit.

171. "Detroit must help to open Japanese market." Tokyo
     Business Today. 60.3 (March 1992): 64.

     This article covers a personal interview with Yutaka
     Kume, president of Nissan Motor Co. and chairman of the
     Japan Automobile Manufacturers Association, concerning
     the relations between U.S. and Japanese auto industries.
     During President Bush's visit, the Japanese auto industry
     agreed to purchase an estimated $19 billion worth of U.S.
     vehicle parts under the condition that these parts meet
     the Japanese standards in terms of cost, quality, and
     keeping on-time dates. As for car sales, Japanese
     automakers agreed to open their dealer networks for the
     U.S. cars. At present, these goals are not realistic
     because there are not enough parts makers in the U.S. to
     supply $19 billion worth of parts, and U.S. companies
     should try to set up their own dealer networks to
     negotiate directly with Japanese car dealers.

172. Flint, Jerry. "Baby steps: a historic step in building
     an export industry." Forbes. 149.8 (April 13, 1992):
     92.

     Detroit is gradually moving towards building a
     manufacturing base for auto exports. This significant
     move marks an historic step for the Big Three in building
     an export industry. General Motors Corp. plans to build
     an Opel minivan for Europe in a U.S. plant. The due date
     is set up in 1995. Japanese plants operating in the U.S.
     also set up their respective export projections for this
     year. The exact figures are detailed in this article.

173. Flint, Jerry. "Alfred Sloan spoken here." Forbes. 148
     (November 11, 1991): 96, 101.

     Alfred Sloan, the auto genius who founded General Motors
     in the 1920s and 1930s, applied his market strategy of
     building a basic automobile structure and redesigning
     several versions around it on GM, has made the company
     the world's biggest and most profitable corporation for
     many years. In adopting Sloan's product development
     strategy, the Japanese build a whole new category of
     semi-luxury cars with lots of power and curve-hugging

ability, such as Honda's Acura Legend, Mitsubishi's
Diamonte, Mazda's 929 and Toyota's ES300. The Big Three
are also upgrading some models to follow the Japanese way
through designing comfortable interiors, adding
equipments to their cars, adjusting car size closest to
the Japanese models, and pushing up prices.

174. Flint, Jerry. "Somebody's wrong." Forbes. 144
    (September 18, 1989): 118.

    While American automakers are reducing production volume,
    Japanese automakers are planning to increase production
    at their U.S. plants without reducing imports. This
    article analyzes the contrasting market strategies
    between the Japanese and American automakers, and the
    aggressive Japanese auto-selling plans in the United
    States.

175. Fujimoto, Hiroshi. "Japan's automobile keiretsu changing
    for the better." Tokyo Business Today. 60.2 (February
    1992): 50-51.

    One of the unique features of the Japan's corporate
    relationships is the so-called "keiretsu," or "group
    affiliation." A great number of Japan's leading auto
    parts suppliers are under the control of automakers.
    While "keiretsu" constitutes a closely-tied system within
    a group, the production format of the world automobile
    industry is changing with the times. Under the current
    demands, "keiretsu" needs to be transformed into a more
    open and global forum for business transactions. The
    Fair Trade Commission has released guidelines concerning
    "keiretsu" dealings. These guidelines are functioned to
    halt price and business domination by big companies.

176. The Future of the automobile: the report of MIT's
    International Automobile Program. Cambridge, MA: The MIT
    Press, 1984.

    Due to the energy crisis in the 1980s, the world economy
    entered the worst economic downturn since the Great
    Depression, and the auto industry went through the most
    severe crisis in the world's recorded history. Research
    institutions in France, Japan, Italy, Sweden, the United
    Kingdom, West Germany, and the United States jointly
    developed and conducted a national research effort which
    was coordinated by MIT's International Automobile Program
    to promote current economic concern and awareness in the
    international auto industry. The present volume is a
    report on the current status of the automobile industry
    and its future prospects based on the findings of the
    program.

177. Gatty, Bob. "Fleet vehicles take a high road." Nation's
    Business. 74.5 (May 1986): 30-32.

    Fleet business has been one good way to raise cash in the
    auto industry. The typical fleet car is a four-cylinder,
    mid-size car with some options offered, such as

air-conditioning and fancy radios.   Domestic models
dominate the market, but some imports, such as high-duty
trucks by Isuzu, and small, compact cars by Toyota, are
recent competitors in the fleet market.

178. "Getting General Motors going again." Economist. (May
     2, 1992): 77-78.

     Hit hard by recession and Japanese imports, Detroit's Big
     Three have experienced a series of auto slumps in recent
     history. Yet, on April 1992 General Motors announced its
     profit gains in the first quarter of this year. This is
     a huge relief for a firm that lost $4.45 billion last
     year. Ford also earned slight gains in the same period.
     Due to the stronger yen and recession, the Japanese
     firms' market share was down from 25.8% in 1991 to 24.5%
     in the first quarter of this year. The author feels that
     with the Japanese expansion in the American market, the
     Big Three's survival (especially for GM) is still far
     from assured.

179. Goto, M. "Productivity, efficiency and cooperation: the
     Japanese   experience."   International   Journal   of
     Technology Management. 1.3/4 (1986): 522-26.

     This paper is a comparative study of the American and
     Japanese auto industries. It discusses the subjects of
     productivity, efficiency, and cooperation from the point
     of view of the Japanese Nissan Motor Co.'s experience.
     Within the last decade, Nissan has gone through dynamic
     changes in structure and management. There are three
     basic goals for the company: 1) be more competitive in
     the   domestic   market;   2)   maintain   leadership   in
     engineering and technology; and 3) make the company more
     international. After that, Nissan opened a transplant in
     Tennessee, and then expanded its facilities in the United
     Kingdom. In the future, Nissan plans to be more involved
     with local plants by providing employment opportunities
     and by purchasing local parts and materials.

180. Gwynne, S. C.   "Running low on gas."   Time.   134.21
     (November 20, 1989): 70-72.

     Describes the troubled automobile industry in the United
     States, and the intense competitions among U.S.,
     Japanese, and European auto companies for car sales in
     the United States.

181. Hage, David and Kevin Chappell.   "Running on empty:
     Detroit's doldrums and Japan's exports threaten U.S. auto
     suppliers." U.S. News & World Report. 111 (August 12,
     1991): 35-37.

     The sharp auto sales slump for Detroit's Big Three within
     recent years was triggered by the domestic auto supply
     industry. As Detroit's auto business faced a downturn,
     these auto suppliers have had no choice but to turn to
     the Japanese automakers in order to survive. But so far,
     the Japanese transplants still prefer doing business with

their long-time suppliers in Japan, or with the local Japanese suppliers that transferred their domestic business abroad. This article describes the current status of the domestic auto supply industry from the perspective of the Japanese transplants in the United States.

182. Henry, Jim. "Low-end luxury sets stage in New York: entry-level BMW, Infiniti make debuts." <u>Automotive News</u>. (April 16, 1990): 4.

Describes the sales campaign between various motor companies for their low-end luxury models. One of them is the sales fight between BMW and Infiniti, as each company introduced a new entry-level model on a New York Auto Show.

183. Higurashi, Ryoichi. "Imported car market begins struggle to survive." <u>Tokyo Business Today</u>. 605 (May 1992): 54-56.

With the slowdown of Japan's overall economics, the market for foreign automobiles in general has lost its advantageous position. Total import car sales for 1991 were down 12.1% from 1990. However, the U.S. car sales grew 5.3%. The sales of General Motors increased 8.8% which was the highest sales ever recorded by GM in Japan. Sales of European cars in Japan also fell in 1991.

184. Hoffman, Kurt and Raphael Kaplinsky. <u>Driving force: the global restructuring of technology, labor, and investment in the automobile and components industries</u>. Boulder, CO: Westview Press, 1988.

This research study analyzes the transformation of the production processes in the manufacture and assembly of automobiles and automobile components, the role of the transnational corporations, and the impact on developing countries. Chapter three and chapter four describe the market condition, manufacturing structure, competitive advantage, and the impact of the VRA (voluntary restraint agreement) on Japanese auto and auto parts industries. Statistical data are included which compare U.S.-Japanese auto trade relations.

185. Horton, Cleveland and Raymond Serafin. "Recovery is good news for U.S. auto marketers." <u>Advertising Age</u>. 63.25 (June 22, 1992): 3, 39.

Domestic vehicles are having a continued but modest recovery as the economy improves, while Japanese automakers are losing market share both at home and abroad. Auto analysts from J.D. Power & Associates discuss three elements which will give domestics the edge in adding business.

186. Iacocca, Lee. "Taking care of business: the Japanese must open their markets." <u>Vital Speeches</u>. 58.10 (March 1, 1992): 295-99.

In a conference presentation delivered by Mr. Lee Iacocca
to the auto industry leaders in Detroit, the topic
focused on the U.S.-Japanese trade relations following
President Bush's recent trade mission to Japan. It was
felt that the trip did not solve the trade problems
encountered between these two countries. Compared to the
auto trade market in America, the Japanese have almost no
competition at home, and they will not allow any foreign
automaker to be a factor in their market. The Japanese
must open their market, and accommodate their entire
economic structure to conform with that of the U.S. and
the rest of the nations.

187. Iacocca, Lee. "Trade with Japan and U.S. economic
     policy." Executive Speeches. 6.10 (May 1992): 6-12.

The President George Bush's visit to Japan accompanied by
the top executives of Big Three has indicated the need
for the Japanese to open trade with the United States.
It is estimated that the foreign automakers worldwide
have only 3% of the Japanese market. However, Japan has
nearly 7 million units of excess auto capacity and most
of it is targeted at the U.S. To deal with the Japanese,
it is necessary for the U.S. automakers to learn the
uniqueness of these problems. Major difficulties lie in
Japan's closed market and Japan's business practices that
affect the U.S. When working with Japan, the U.S. should
focus on results not on process. One of the results
which the U.S. should pay attention to is employment.

188. Inaba, Yu and Mikio Tsutsui. "Japanese car market
     up-scale drive." Tokyo Business Today. 58.5 (May 1990):
     50-53.

Japanese automobile market keeps expanding in mid-1990s,
and a major change is taking place in the level of
quality. Sales of upscale cars are strong with the
introduction of Toyota's Lexus LS400 and Nissan's
Infiniti Q45 models. Families that own multiple vehicles
are common place, and more new models come to market to
lure second car buyers and to satisfy baby boomers'
youthful tastes. Ford Motor Co. continues joint ventures
with Japan, called Autorama. Many U.S. automakers are
just trying desperately to gain market shares in Japan.
Their efforts are not quite successful due to the
Japanese closed nature to foreign automakers, and trade
barriers between these two countries.

189. Ingrassia, Paul. "Auto industry in U.S. is sliding
     relentlessly into Japanese hands." Wall Street Journal.
     (February 16, 1990): A1, A5.

The relationship of U.S. and Japanese auto industries and
Japan's growing dominance of the American auto industry
are fully discussed. Japan captured a record 26% of U.S
auto sales in 1989. Entering the 1990s, the automotive
competition between these two countries is as vibrant as
ever. The American Big Three keep falling behind in auto
sales while the Japanese rivals' auto profits and global

market share continue to grow.   This situation caused
Detroit to expand its operations to Europe.   But the
Japanese also stretched their arms into European
countries.   Auto experts predict that by the year 2000,
Japan's combined profits in the U.S. and Europe will take
40% of global sales, up from 28% in 1990.   At the same
time, Detroit's share will drop to 28% from 35% during
the same period.   Detroit's automakers continue to narrow
the quality and cost gaps.   The Japanese challenge and
automotive competition in the U.S. will be tense in the
years to come.

190. "Japan has a new lesson for Detroit."   Business Week.
     3184 (October 22, 1990): 128.

This article discusses the strengths and weaknesses of
the American and Japanese auto markets on quality issues.

191. "Japan-bashing: where the jobs are." Economist. 322.7744
     (February 1, 1992): 25-26.

The impact of economic recession on the ailing American
auto industry, especially on the concentrated automaking
states in the Great Lake region is described.   Except for
the state of Michigan, much of the region has done well
by the Japanese cars.   For the past ten years, Japan's
share of the U.S. car sales has grown from 28% in 1980 to
31% by 1991.   Over half of the sales came from the
Japanese transplants built in America. At present, there
are eight transplants established in America, five of
them are located in the Great Lake region.   These plants
absorbed much of the labor force from the local
residents, and their impacts on the Great Lake region
were great in terms of job market, local business,
cultural diversity and labor-management relations between
the Japanese workforce and local residents.

192. "Japanese automakers' sweet success."   Journal of
     Commerce and Commercial. (December 21, 1989): 10a.

Even with seven plants in the United States, four plants
in Canada, and a total 2.6 million cars per year capacity
in those two countries, Japanese automakers are still
feeling the wave of competition from the United States
auto industry.   Japanese companies make 1.2 million cars
per year in the U.S. and export another 2.3 million cars
to the U.S. from Japan. This could give their cars a 30%
market share in the United States, versus the present
25%.

193. "Japanese car makers aiming for U.S. sales of over 2.8
     million units in FY 1990."   Comline Transportation.
     (January 26, 1990), 2.

Car sales and consumption figures show that U.S. sales of
Japanese cars are likely to reach 2.85 million units in
fiscal year 1990.   For the next fiscal year, demand for
Japanese vehicles is estimated to increase.   It will make

up over a 30% share of the U.S. car market, from the
current level of 26%.

194. "Japanese drive a hard bargain on emissions standards."
     CQ. (January 20, 1990): 164-65.

     The debate on whether to require all automakers to meet
     the same fleet-wide miles-per-gallon (mpg) targets or to
     require percentage measure based on each manufacturer's
     1988 fuel economy has positioned the Japanese against
     Detroit's Big Three. In contrast to the Japanese
     automakers and dealers who prefer to keep the current mpg
     formula, U.S. automakers would rather choose a percentage
     measure of fuel economy. The issue of revising the
     current corporate average fuel economy (CAFE) standards
     is discussed.

195. Jefferies, Francis M. "Automobile and automotive parts
     industry."   In Understanding the Japanese industrial
     challenge: from automobiles to software.   Francis M.
     Jefferies.   Poolesville, MD: Jefferies & Associates,
     Inc., 1987, pp. 181-94.

     This chapter gives a brief account of the automotive and
     automotive parts industry, particularly from the point of
     view of trade figures of Japanese imports into the United
     States.   It also shows possible reasons for trade
     advantages and the analysis of cost and productivity
     between the United States and Japanese auto companies.
     The last part of the chapter contains suggested
     improvement goals and policies for U.S. manufacturers and
     government.

196. Kannan, Narasimhan, Kathy K. Rebribo and Donna L. Ellis.
     Downsizing Detroit: the future of the United States
     automobile industry. New York, NY: Praeger, 1982.

     1980 was the worst year in the history of the American
     automobile industry.   The energy crisis and the
     associated economic turmoil of the 1970s accelerated the
     gradual decline of auto production in the United States.
     This book presents an overview of these problems;
     analyzes U. S. labor costs and the consequences of long
     term production decline; and discusses the alternate
     short-term transition policies such as import quotas, job
     training, regulatory reform, and management remedies,
     using Japanese standards of inventory control, quality
     control, and labor relations as role models.

197. Keller, Maryann.   "Are we really closing the gap?"
     Chilton's Automotive Industries. (July 1989): 13.

     The debate over achieving international competitiveness
     in automaking between Japan and the United States is the
     central theme of this article. Several important factors
     contributed to this discussion which include automobile
     quality, manufacturing productivity, workers' wages,
     salaries, benefits, and employment security, and pension
     expenses for retirees.

198. Kerwin, Kathleen, et al. "Detroit's big chance: can it regain business and respect it lost in the past 20 years?" Business Week. 3272 (June 29, 1992): 82-90.

The Big Three's profits are coming back. The American automakers gained 72.4% of the domestic car and light-truck market in the first five months of 1992, up 1.6 points from a year ago. The Japanese lost 1.4 points, to 24% for the same period. American cars now lead the Japanese in fuel economy and safety features. Improved product quality and reduced production cycles will help Detroit to regain some of the businesses. Auto analysts agree that this is a good chance for the Big Three. In the long run, a resurgent Detroit might help revitalize U.S. manufacturing.

199. Law, Christopher M., ed. Restructuring the global automobile industry: national and regional impact. London ; New York, NY: Routledge, 1991.

This book consists of twelve papers submitted by the lecturers of the Institute of British Geographers' Industrial Activity and Area Development Study Group at an annual conference held in January 1989, in Coventry, London. The papers focus on the growing importance and role of Japanese companies in the industry. Each paper covers one subject discussion, such as: motor vehicle manufacturing, the world automotive industry, the Third World motor vehicle industry, the industrial structure and technical evolution of the Japanese automobile industry, the impact of Japanese investment in the U.S., motor components industry, and the case studies of the motor vehicle industry in Coventry, London; Austin Rover in Longbridge, Birmingham, and in the West Midlands.

200. Levin, Doron P. "Car buyers turn back to Detroit." New York Times. (August 11, 1992): D1, D5.

Through years of cost-cutting and improving productivity, Detroit seems to be finally paying off in the automobile industry. During the first half of 1992, the Big Three took 71.9% share of the 6.5 million cars and trucks sold in the United States, a 1.7% growth rate from a year earlier. There are several reasons to explain this: 1) buy-American fervor went up in January during President Bush's visit in Japan; 2) Japanese automakers have raised prices due to the dollar's weakness against yen; and 3) facts about quality and value have lead to some powerful rethinking of domestics versus imports.

201. Levin, Doron P. "For Detroit, time to buckle down." New York Times. (January 13, 1992): D1, D5.

Heightened by token concessions and minor relief from President Bush's visit to Japan, the U.S. auto industry became an issue of central debate. It's time for Detroit to seek its own strategies to compete with foreign automakers, especially the Japanese. This article analyzes the weakness of the U.S. auto industry from three different angles: auto-manufacturing, engineering and design, and marketing strategies.

202. Levin, Doron P.   "Parts pact with Japan may backfire." New York Times.   (February 3, 1992): D1, D3.

The proposed agreement made by Japanese automakers with U.S. Government officials on raising the purchasing volume of U.S.-made parts from $10 billion in 1990 to $19 billion by 1994 was debated by U.S. automakers. On the U.S. side, the uncertainty over how the agreement will play out is the most disturbing thing for U.S. automakers. This article describes the U.S.-Japanese automaking relationship and compares the relations between automakers and suppliers in both countries.

203. Levin, Doron P.   "U.S. sales of vehicles jump 23.9%: Detroit gains share from Japan rivals." New York Times. (July 7, 1992): D1, D6.

The U.S. auto industry reported a strong sales jump of 23.9% in the last ten days of June 1992, compared with the same period a year earlier. The Big Three's auto sales rose sharply in late June. Sales of General Motors' domestically produced cars jumped 18.4%, Ford rose 30.7%, and Chrysler's light-truck sales rose 23.1% for the entire month of June. However, Chrysler's car sales in June declined 12.2%. Because of America's stronger position in light trucks than the Japanese, the Big Three have gained significantly in the overall market share. In the meantime, Japanese automakers felt the sales pinch in their auto-manufacturing business in America. Sales of both Toyota and Honda cars dropped for the month, and only Nissan's car sales enjoyed a steady increase with 13.4% rise in the month of June.

204 Levin, Doron P.   "Honda ready to show a car that gets 100 miles a gallon." New York Times. (October 17, 1991): D1, D5.

Just as Congress is ready to debate a new energy bill that could include tougher corporate average fuel efficiency (CAFE) standards for vehicles sold in America, Honda's EP-X, a high-mileage, two-seat passenger car whose fuel efficiency could top nearly 100 miles a gallon, is displayed at the recent Tokyo Motor Show. The debate on tougher CAFE standards is likely to stir strong opposing views from both Japanese and American automakers.

205. Levin, Doron P.   "An auto glut that won't go away." New York Times.   (July 29, 1991): 1, 6.

With great fanfare, Chrysler Corp. announced the opening of its new plant facility on Jefferson Ave., Detroit. Most people have mixed feelings for this. In one way, it marks Detroit's determination to catch and surpass the Japanese. But it also compounds the ailing American auto industry: the problem of overcapacity. As production capacity keeps growing, while industry sales continue to shrink, this situation has heightened competition for market share and marketing wars between the Japanese and American automakers. Capacity utilization rates at plants in both countries are also under scrutiny. In general, Japanese plants here have roughly the same or a little higher utilization rates than American plants. The Big Three plan to close more plants in the near future to strike a balance between capacity and demand.

206. Lieberman, Marvin B., Lawrence J. Lau and Mark D. Williams. "Firm-level productivity and management influence: a comparison of U.S. and Japanese automobile producers." Management Science. 36.10 (October 1990): 1193-1215.

This study compares the productivity and management of six major U.S. and Japanese auto manufacturers: General Motors, Ford, Chrysler, Toyota, Nissan, and Mazda, from the early 1950s through 1987. The results show that productivity improvement in the auto industry has been attained primarily through more efficient utilization of labor. All three Japanese producers have attained labor advantages over their U.S. counterparts. The adoption of the "just-in-time" system has also contributed to productivity gains in both countries.

207. Lohr, Steve. "Ford and Chrysler outpace Japanese in reducing costs." New York Times. (June 18, 1992): D1-D2.

This paper discusses the productivity improvements at Ford Motor Co. and Chrysler Corp. and compares the cost efficiencies of car production between American and Japanese auto industries.

208. Maital, Shlomo. "The next round." Across the Board. (July-August 1992): 48-49.

This paper addresses the competitiveness of the American automobile industry, describes causes of the industry's weakness, and suggests remedies for the ailing American auto industry. The author compares the production statistics of U.S. and Japanese auto industries between 1985 and 1991, analyzes the quality and capacity factors of auto productions from these two countries, and provides suggestions to save the future U.S. automobile industry.

209. Maskery, Mary Ann. "Japan prepares for stiffer U.S. rules on air, CAFE." Automotive News. (February 26, 1990): 6.

The central theme of this article is the reaction of the Japanese auto industry to the corporate average fuel economy (CAFE) and emissions debate in Congress. In order to meet U.S. government standards, Japanese automakers have taken action by increasing the use of multi-valve engines, optimizing fuel mixtures, improving

ignition timing, changing to electronic fuel injection,
adopting 3-way catalysts, reducing friction in the engine
and using lighter parts in pistons. No matter how strict
the future government regulations will be, Japanese
automakers will always be prepared to take those rules
into very serious consideration.

210. Maxcy, George. The multinational automobile industry.
     New York, NY: St. Martin's Press, 1981.

     This book is an automobile industry study of
     multinational enterprises. Part one provides a
     theoretical framework for the auto industry in general.
     In part two, the overall motor industry development and
     growth is traced from the early 20th century to the
     present. The case studies of automobile development in
     Japan, the United States, and several other countries are
     described in part three.

211. "Mazda motor: Mazda announces plans to promote global
     business partnerships." Japan 21st. (April 1992):
     21-30.

     The company updates of Mazda Motor Corp. are covered.
     They include the following: 1) Mazda's new plan to
     promote cooperative relationships with foreign companies
     and increased purchasing of foreign products; 2) the
     introduction of MX-6, a sports specialty coupe, to the
     Japanese market; 3) the release of Eunos 500, a new
     high-quality sedan, in Japan; and 4) the start-up
     operations at its new Hofu plant primarily for luxury
     models.

212. McElroy, John. "R&D spending comparison: why do Japanese
     automakers have a sparkling reputation for innovation?"
     Chilton's Automotive Industries. 172.4 (April 1992):
     46-48.

     An analysis of the worldwide automotive research and
     development indicates that Japanese automakers put
     proportionately more resources into R&D than the
     Europeans or Americans. The Japanese auto companies are
     also capable of designing new products or building new
     factories for much less investment than Western
     companies. This article offers a detailed review of R&D
     spending comparison between leading Japanese automakers
     (Toyota, Honda and Nissan) and the American Big Three
     (General Motors, Ford and Chrysler) within the 1980-1991
     period.

213. Miller, Annetta and Frank Washington. "Can the Big Three
     get back in gear?" Newsweek. 115 (January 22, 1990):
     42-43.

     This article describes the contemporary auto designs of
     U.S. and Japanese models, and analyzes the recent
     technology involved in making these cars. The market
     competition of U.S. and Japanese automobiles and the

problematic state of the Big three, as well as suggested
catch-up plans, are offered at the end of this paper.

214. Miller, Karen Lowry. "What's this? American cars gaining
     in Japan?" Business Week. 3223 (July 22, 1991): 82-83.

Although American cars are still rare in Japan, they
attract a growing number of royal customers. Detroit's
sales have climbed since 1985, and 1991 sales could top
1979s record of 16,709 units. Detroit's automakers are
now taking gradual steps toward promoting and developing
their products in order to compete with Japanese
automobiles.

215. Mitchell, Jacqueline. "GM's price strategy for 1993
     reflects Detroit bid to squeeze Japanese rivals." Wall
     Street Journal. (August 14, 1992): B1.

Pressured by economic slowdown both at home and abroad,
Japanese automakers have raised prices sharply in the
past few months. U.S. automakers are taking advantage of
this by raising the price of their 1993 models with a
moderate 2% to 6% but holding the line or cutting prices
on some aging and less successful models. Detroit's
executives are confident that the steep Japanese prices
will result in a loss of market share by the Japanese.

216. "More cars than drivers: Japanese carmakers head for
     trouble." Economist. 313.7629 (November 18, 1989):
     76-78.

Problems do exist in the Japanese auto market. During
the first ten months of 1989, Japanese auto sales had an
11% increase over last year, but the market is expected
to decline. The expansion plans in Europe were slowed
because of the political pressure there. Japanese trade
surplus versus the U.S. trade deficit was another problem
which was waiting to be solved. Japan's Ministry of
International Trade and Industry has already taken
actions and remedial measures to try to solve all these
problems.

217. Moskal, Brian S. "Auto preview: just put your lips
     together and blow." Industry Week. 238.20 (October 16,
     1989): 24-28.

The auto market in 1990 is driven by value, quality,
styling, and incentives in order to fit consumer taste.
The domestic auto company is raising prices to ensure
higher rebates for market attraction. The Japanese are
not doing so because of the appreciation of yen against
the strengthening dollar. The main issue for 1990 is the
potential increase in the foreign sponsored share of the
American auto market. With the arrival of two luxury
cars, Toyota's Lexus and Nissan's Infiniti, the current
competition would be even tougher for the U.S. auto
industry.

218. Moskal, Brian S. "Tilt in the sector: autos." Industry
     Week. 241.10 (May 18, 1992): 24-26.

     Compared with Toyota's Lexus which sells for $44,300 in
     the U.S., Chrysler Jeep Cherokee bears a sticker price
     as high as $44,000 in Japan. There are many other
     examples of American-made vehicles that carry a much
     stiffer price tag in Japan than they do in the U.S. This
     situation explains why U.S. automakers can not easily get
     their products into the Japanese market because of
     distinctive price disadvantages. The major barriers to
     the Japanese market include government inspection and
     certification fees, overseas freight and customs
     clearance, sales tax, and the cost of distribution and
     dealer margins. American cars account for only 0.4% of
     the Japanese market, however, 30% share of the U.S. auto
     market is dominated by Japanese manufacturers.

219. Moskal, Brian S. "Detroit: can it learn 'new' math?"
     Industry Week. 239.19 (October 1, 1990): 28-35.

     Japanese automakers in the United States will soon reach
     the capacity of producing 2.3 million units per year.
     This is a big warning sign for Detroit's business in the
     1990s. Several factors could explain the current
     situation for the Big Three: corporate downsizing,
     lengthy products' cycle, and poor quality control.
     Japanese materials take shorter product cycles than
     American products, and in general, their products'
     quality is better. They have the ability to make money
     with less than 200,000 units of a single model per year,
     but American companies cannot. Human motivation and
     employee respect are also important. Ford, General
     Motors, and Chrysler are now changing their attitudes to
     put major emphasis on people, and also re-evaluate their
     market strategies, quality control methods, and
     customers' tastes. The domestic auto industry can no
     longer keep up with the global market by doing things in
     the old way. They need to catch up with Japanese
     competition in the 1990s.

220. Odaka, Konosuke, ed. The Motor vehicle industry in Asia:
     a study of ancillary firm development. [Singapore]:
     Published for Council for Asian Manpower Studies, by
     Singapore University Press, 1983.

     This research study investigates primarily the
     possibility that foreign, up-to-date, technology is
     transferred effectively to the local machine industry
     sector through the growing linkages between the potential
     primary and the indigenous ancillary firms. Japan is one
     of the six Asian countries being discussed. The major
     issues of discussion include technology, management,
     market, growth process of the firm, exploitation aspects,
     and government policy measures.

221. "Offshore content to reach 28% by 1985 OEM, supplier
     study predicts." Ward's Automotive Reports. (September
     2, 1985): 274-75.

According to the Reports, 28% of foreign motor vehicle parts will be imported by 1995, versus 23% in 1990. Japan will be the leading source with an 8-10% share of the total U.S. market. By 1995, some 1.1 million foreign cars will be assembled in the United States. Domestic models will account for only 60% of the market.

222. Okochi, Akio and Koichi Shimokawa. <u>Development of mass marketing: the automobile and retailing industries; proceedings of the Fuji Conference</u>. [Tokyo]: University of Tokyo Press, 1981.

This book treats the subject of marketing in several countries from a historical standpoint, with particular reference to the automobile as a common denominator. The main discussion is concerned with the comparative study of the development of marketing for the marketing history in the automobile industry of the United States and Japan. One chapter covers Japanese automobile marketing from the historical origin, its consolidation, development, and characteristics. Others cover the origin and development of automobile marketing in the following countries: Britain, France, Germany, and the United States.

223. Passell, Peter. "Car wars: more bad news." <u>New York Times</u>. (June 26, 1991): D2.

Discusses the gap in brand loyalty between American and Japanese automobiles. According to the Mannering-Winston analysis, the gap actually means that Detroit's Big Three will continue to lose sales to the Japanese automakers. Before 1980, loyalty to both brands was about the same. But after 1980, loyalty rates changed. Japan's share of the American auto market tended to rise sharply. This signifies that sales of U.S.-made cars will continue to decline.

224. Pemberton, Max. <u>The world car industry to the year 2000</u>. London: The Economist Intelligence Unit, 1988.

This report analyzes the world market size and demand for automobiles, attempts to provide detailed information on auto developments based on the statistical data compiled from 171 countries concerning annual sales volumes and vehicles in use since 1960, and assesses the probable structure and view of the passenger car industry in the period up to the year 2000.

225. Penzer, Erika. "Selling service: lessons from America." <u>Incentive</u>. 163.11 (November 1989): 30-34.

Japanese companies usually put customer service on a low priority because of their high demand on car sales and their relatively low supplies on cars. On the contrary, the American car makers, faced with declining sales, embraced customer service as a last resort against losing buyers. Companies such as General Motors, Ford and Chevrolet have developed extensive programs. Nissan,

Honda, and Mitsubishi are now following up with sales
incentive programs and customer satisfaction services.

226. Phillips, Richard, Arthur Way and A. T. Lowry, et al.
     Auto industries of Europe, U.S. and Japan. Cambridge,
     MA: Abt Associates, 1982.

     The U.S. auto industry used to be the world's leading
     automobile producer, but since 1980, it was overtaken by
     Japan as the world's largest automaker. This book
     provides some insights into the future direction of the
     automotive industries of the U.S., Western Europe, and
     Japan, and analyzes the different but related problems
     faced by each of these countries in an attempt to predict
     some of the strategies they will adopt to meet the
     economic challenges of the 1980s.

227. "Propping up Detroit." Economist. 7746 (February 15,
     1992): 75-76.

     A campaign commissioned by the Economic Strategy
     Institute on providing the Big Three with appropriate
     protective measures against foreign competition is being
     promoted in Detroit. The main issue focuses on the
     differences of production costs between American and
     Japanese cars. The value represents a true gap in
     capacity costs, health costs, labor costs, and capital
     costs between the automobile industries in both
     countries.

228. Rader, James. Penetrating the U.S. auto market: German
     and Japanese strategies, 1965-1976. Ann Arbor, MI: UMI
     Research Press, 1980.

     The purpose of this study is to describe, analyze, and
     evaluate the marketing strategies employed by Japanese
     and German automakers in penetrating the American market
     with particular emphasis placed on the developmental
     aspects of these strategies. There are three major
     structural elements of this study: a survey of the
     literature of corporate, marketing, and multinational
     strategies; a description of product and market scope;
     and analysis of the firms' overall marketing strategies.
     The effectiveness and efficiency of each firm's
     penetration of the American market is evaluated to
     determine the firm's degree of strategic success.

229. Rescigno, Richard. "Spinning their wheels: the Big Three
     auto makers face a long, hard road." Barron's. 71.2
     (January 14, 1991): 14-18.

     In an interview, Maryann Keller, an automotive analyst
     and author of the book Rude awakening: the rise, fall and
     struggle for recovery of General Motors, analyzed the
     current trend of the automobile industry and emphasized
     that both the cyclical and secular effects should be
     judged for the whole auto industry field. She predicted
     that auto business would eventually go back to normal
     after the recession. Several ways were used to

compensate their losses. Car rental programs offered a
unique solution to benefit both sides. Cost-cutting and
cash rebates provided another means of financial
releases. The present business situation of the Big
Three and the status of the Japanese companies,
especially Toyota's operations in the U.S., were fully
discussed.

230. Rescigno, Richard. "Fasten your seats belts: the auto
makers may be in for their hardest race yet." Barron's.
70.29 (July 16, 1990): 10-11, 20-29.

In a panel discussion assembled by Barron's, four leading
experts of the auto industry discussed the auto market
trend over the next few years in comparison with the
present business situation in the United States, Japan,
and Europe. They talked about the auto sales of Big
Three, quality control issues, problems of
competitiveness among U.S. and Japanese auto industries,
marketing strategies, impact of emission standards and
clean air legislation, joint ventures, and business
potential in the Eastern European market.

231. Rhys, D. G. The motor industry: an economic survey.
London: Butterworth, 1972.

The following areas are dealt with at length in this
volume: the historical development and structure of the
motor industry; overseas automobile industry development,
including Europe, North America, Japan, and other new
car-producing countries; the supply and demand of the
products; and the nature of competition, exports, and
labor relations in the industry. In chapter six, the
rudimentary structure and early development of Japan's
auto industry is fully described. The author utilizes
the available statistical and econometric data to support
his theories and thoughts in this book.

232. Rudolph, Barbara. "Auto suppliers." Forbes. 31 (January
3, 1983): 144-45.

The growing presence of Japanese transplant operations in
the United States is a real challenge for American parts
suppliers. At first, American parts suppliers were
confident that they would profit from Japanese auto
plants in the U.S. In fact, there seems to be a lot more
threat than promise in them. Japanese auto parts
companies generally hold long-term affiliations with
their manufacturers. Unless they are forced to buy
American parts under local content legislation, they
would prefer to buy parts from their long-term affiliated
suppliers. The U.S. auto parts industry should
demonstrate better quality and productivity in order to
meet with the Japanese challenge.

233. Sanger, David E. "In Japan's view, U.S. car companies
should be blaming only themselves." New York Times.
(January 6, 1992): A12.

This article analyzes the American auto industry as it compared to the Japanese auto industry today. Several major differences or key issues were brought up in this report, which include: 1) the American automakers failed to make large investments on new products that have brought success in both the domestic and foreign markets; 2) the Big Three ignored market needs for the Japanese consumers with cars that are of the right size and right feel for them; and 3) Detroit should be more aggressive on building its own design centers in Japan, just like its rival Japanese people that deliberately established their assembly plants and auto design centers in this country.

234. Sanger, David E. "Japanese cars stronger in weak U.S. economy." New York Times. (September 4, 1991): D1, D3.

During the first half year of 1991, Japanese automakers have gained almost 30% of the U.S. market share, the growth of more than 4% since 1989. Japanese manufacturers attributed their success to the marketing of upscale models like Honda's Acura and Toyota's Lexus line. Other Japanese companies also followed by introducing Nissan's Infiniti, and Mitsubishi's Diamonte. Basically, auto manufacturers from both sides followed completely different recession strategies. The Japanese used the recession to rebuild their capacity, while the Big Three tended to wait for the recession to pass by.

235. Sanger, David E. "U.S. slump hurts Japan car sales." New York Times. (March 4, 1991): D1.

The economic downturn in the Untied States and an unusual trend of frugality among Japanese consumers finally start to hurt Japan's leading automobile manufacturers, forcing them to cut production and rebuild plans for continuous expansion in the American market.

236. Schlossberg, Howard. "Carmakers try to boost sales by satisfying buyers." Marketing News. 24.11 (May 28, 1990): 2,11,19.

In 1989, Japan occupied 25% of the total U.S. auto market. The Big Three had a combined 67% only. In 1990, Big Three sales were down 1.5% compared to a year earlier. The major factors for the Japanese success are customer satisfaction and quality of products. Japanese cars are easily adapted to the U.S. market since they are more fuel efficient, smaller in size, and good in quality. However, the U.S. automakers are getting nowhere near the penetration in Japan because of the Japanese trade restrictions, and the unfavorable reaction to the larger size and less fuel-efficient American cars. For these reasons, U.S. automakers are working to improve quality and are focusing on Europe for new markets. At the present time, the Big three still rely heavily on rebates, special financing rates, and other promotional measures in their marketing strategies.

237. Sekaly, Raymond. <u>Transnationalization of the automotive industry</u>. Ottawa, Canada: University of Ottawa Press, 1981.

There are three parts in this book which mainly describe the multinational automotive firms and its subsidiaries located in various nations. In part one, the book covers the structure of the automotive industry in a global sense and describes its current market status and auto supply needs. Part two contains the industrial policy of automobile manufacturers from the following countries: the U.S., Great Britain, France, Italy, Federal Republic of Germany, and Japan. The relative management strategies and import-export policies are explained. Part three concentrates on the transnationalization of this industry, the overall production and world trade figures of the products.

238. Serafin, Raymond and Patricia Strnad. "Chrysler to take on Japan." <u>Advertising Age</u>. 61.8 (February 19, 1990): 1,72.

This article describes the current business condition of Chrysler Motor Corp., the corporate strategies delivered by Chairman Lee Iacocca, and Japanese competition with the company.

239. Siegel, Stewart. "The new models for 1991: light truck Class 1-2." <u>Fleet Owner</u>. 85.7 (July 1990): 59-64.

For most Class 1-2 vehicles and chassis manufacturers, the 1991 models of light-duty trucks will be the suitable models to serve commercial-fleet utility, service, and delivery needs in the under-10,000-lb. category. New models produced by General Motors, Ford, Isuzu, Mitsubishi, and Nissan are announced and their utility functions are described in this article.

240. Sinclair, Stuart W. <u>The world car: the future of the automobile industry</u>. New York, NY: Facts on File Publications, 1983.

This book relates the major crisis faced in the car industry during the 1970s, namely the scarcity of oil and postwar economic recession which caused a severe drop of auto production. It further describes the situation of the international car industry in the 1970s with the eclipse of the European market and the growth of Japanese exports. A global overview of the automobile industry in the 1980s, the future market trend, the outlook for sales to 1985, and international competition are covered on the last part of this book.

241. Singleton, Christopher J. "Auto industry jobs in the 1980's: a decade of transition." <u>Monthly Labor Review</u>. 115.2 (February 1992): 18-27.

This article presents an historical overview of the American auto market with major emphasis on factors that influenced productivity and employment rates during the decade of 1980s. The primary factors of these include: fierce competition and high cyclical demand from foreign automakers during the 1980s, and the impact of oil shocks in 1973 and 1979 that resulted in growing demand for more fuel-efficient Japanese cars. This article describes and analyzes these competitive pressures faced by U.S. automakers and discusses future economic development and employment requirements of the American automobile industry.

242. Smitka, Michael J. Competitive ties: subcontracting in the Japanese automotive industry. New York, NY: Columbia University Press, 1991.

This study covers an extensive analysis of Japanese subcontracting, its benefit on the Japanese auto transplant business, the evolution of subcontracting practice, and its perspectives. The sign of Japanese automobile business success in the United States suggests strongly that the Japanese management style, strategic planning, and labor relations are all major factors behind their firms' practices. The Japanese strategic alliances among automakers and their suppliers depend on mutual trust and cooperative relationships. Thus subcontracting plays a vital role within the Japanese auto industry. Two case studies are covered in this book: 1) the Soja Industrial Park, the auto components supplier of Mizushima Assembly Plant of Mitsubishi Motors; and 2) three "secondary" subcontractors (firms without direct ties to an auto company): the Kato Shatai Group, Kato Shantai Kogyo, and Suzuki Banken.

243. Sobel, Robert. Car wars: the untold story. New York, NY: E.P. Dutton, 1984.

This books includes three parts. Part one describes the history of the American automobile industry from 1950 to 1980, analyzes the rise of Ford, General Motors, and Chrysler, and addresses the development and prosperity of the United States auto industry. Part two focuses on the Japanese auto market, with descriptions of the industrial development of the major Japanese auto companies, including Toyota, Nissan, Honda, Fuji, and Toyo Kogyo (Mazda). Comparative studies of the U.S.-Japanese auto management strategies and descriptions of their striving for success in the American market are also covered. Financial statistics and economic analyses were used to support the author's theories in this book. Suggestions and prospects for the future of the auto industry are found in part three of this book.

244. Strnad, Patricia. "On edge in the middle of America." Advertising Age. 63 (March 30, 1992): S24, S38.

The primary reason for Japanese automakers to build plants in America's Midwest is to capture sales from domestic brands. So far, all of the leading Japanese auto manufacturers have built factories in the Midwest.

They include Toyota Motor Corp., Honda Motor Corp., Nissan Motor Co., Mazda Motor Corp., Mitsubishi Motors Corp. and a joint venture by Fuji Heavy Industries and Isuzu Motors.

245. Takahashi, Kazuko. "What you want is not always what you get from the U.S." Japan Times. 32.10 (March 9-15, 1992): 8.

In an effort to reduce the over $43 billion U.S.-Japan trade imbalance, the major Japanese auto manufacturers have unveiled an action plan to call for export targets of 20,000 American cars per year and $19 billion sales in the United States or imports to Japan of U.S.-made auto parts. This plan, however, would run in contravention of what Japanese consumers really want to get from the United States. In order to gain a better understanding of Japanese markets and increase profitability, American companies should consider joint partnerships with Japanese corporations.

246. Taylor, Alex III. "U.S. cars come back." Fortune. 126.11 (November 16, 1992): 52-85.

Under the growing competitive pressure from Japan, the American automobile industry has operated with reduced profits and lowered market shares for nearly a decade. With an economic downturn at home and abroad, for the first time in a decade, the U.S. auto industry grasps the chance of beating the Japanese competition. This article is based on comprehensive interviews with industry executives, consultants, academics, and auto analysts in the U.S. and Japan. It covers detailed historical and industrial analyses of the U.S. and Japanese auto industries and highlights the management lessons that emerge from a close reading of the past decade's automobile history.

247. Taylor, Alex III. "Iacocca talks on what ails Detroit." Fortune. 121.4 (February 12, 1990): 68-72.

In an interview with Chrysler Chairman Lee Iacocca, the discussions centered around the U.S. economy, Japanese competition, and Chrysler's need to strengthen its ties with overseas automakers in the 1990s. The auto sales slump of the Big Three could be reversed if the combination of continuing rebates and cutting back production were applied. Mr. Iacocca acknowledged that the Japanese built good quality cars because they emphasized product quality and fuel economy. However, the perception has persisted among the American people that Japanese cars are better. This perception should be changed. U.S. car makers could change that perception by maintaining high quality and by being a low-cost producer.

248. Taylor, Alex III. "Japan's new U.S. car strategy." Fortune. 122.6 (September 10, 1990): 65-80.

This article presents a complete overview and analysis of Japan's new U.S. car strategy, its future directions, and continental marketing plans. It starts with the current status and activities of Japanese auto companies operating in the United States. The Japanese began as exporters of their own cars; their next move was to assemble the cars in America. Today, Honda, Toyota, and Nissan are well on their way to becoming nearly autonomous producers. The Japanese expect to develop more models exclusively for fitting the American taste. Their success is attributed to the following major factors: marketing acumen, efficient development time, low operating cost, and high quality standards. After successful competition in the U.S. auto market, their next move will be to Western Europe, and then gradual expansion to Asia. In the long term, Detroit needs to challenge the Japanese world-wide.

249. Taylor, Alex III. "Why U.S. carmakers are losing ground." Fortune. 120.9 (October 23, 1989): 96-116.

This article describes the business situation of the Big Three and analyzes the major factors which led to the success of the Japanese auto business. They are summarized as follows: good product quality, superior labor-management relations, greater worker involvement, cost-advantages on labor, wages, and fringe benefits, lower defects rate, and more frequent redesign cycles.

250. "Teaming with ideas." Economist. 306.7539 (February 27, 1988): 55.

The Japanese auto industry was emerged from a net importer of technology in 1980 into a net exporter by 1985. Their car manufacturers have turned themselves into some of the most productive inventors in the global auto industry. The secret of their success is a unique approach to management and organization. Comparison of U.S. and Japanese R&D efforts is discussed.

251. Templeman, John. "Infiniti and Lexus: characters in a German nightmare (They're threatening the luxury-car stranglehold of BMW and Mercedes)." Business Week. (October 9, 1989): 64.

This article points out how the invasion of Japan's Infiniti and Lexus on the European auto market threatened Germany's luxury car business, especially represented by the profit-making of Daimler-Benz, BMW, and Porsche for their dominant position of the past several decades. Quality, price, successful marketing strategy, and strong government support are the best assets of Japanese automobiles. The European auto market is certainly prepared to face this challenge now.

252. Thomas, Robert Paul. An analysis of the pattern of growth of the automobile industry, 1895-1929. New York, NY: Arno Press, 1977.

The historical growth pattern of the automobile industry from its rudimentary stage year of 1895 to the advent of the Great Depression in 1929 is the coverage of this study. It describes in general the early history of world automobile development, the growth and expansion years from 1908 to 1918, and the tumbling years during the beginning of the twentieth century.

253. Tolliday, Steven and Jonathan Zeitlin. The Automobile industry and its workers: between Fordism and flexibility. New York, NY: St. Martin's Press, 1987.

This book covers the development of the automobile industry from its origins to the present including the current upheavals in markets, technology, and industrial relations. It is divided into three parts. Part one investigates the rise of mass production and the modification of the Fordist model. Part two focuses on global variations in trade-union structure, bargaining strategy and job-control practices. The industrial relations and union strategies applied either from the universal point of view, in the United States and France, or in the Japanese case Toyota, separately, are discussed. In part three, it traces the recent transformations in the international automobile industry, and marks the implications for industrial relations and trade-union strategy.

254. Toy, Stewart. "Carmakers are doing their dreaming in California." Business Week. (March 30, 1987): 50-52.

Japanese carmakers have been quietly building auto design centers in Southern California since 1973. Right now there are eleven car companies which have opened their design studios in California. They include Japanese carmakers: Toyota, Nissan, Honda, Mazda, Mitsubishi, Isuzu, and Subaru; plus Ford, GM, Chrysler, and Volvo. The Japanese "Americanization" strategy is geared to creating cars strictly for the U.S. market. Besides, California is the home of the top design schools in the United States. Such targeted marketing could make Japanese automakers even tougher competitors than they are already.

255. Transnational corporations in the international auto industry. New York, NY: United Nations, 1983.

This report is the result of the study done by the United Nations Center on Transnational Corporations (TNCs). It covers the following areas: the production and market analysis of the international auto industry; the role of transnational corporations (TNCs) in the auto industry; and the impact of these TNCs on developing countries. Japanese based auto transnational corporations are covered in chapter two. The following major Japanese firms with overseas assembly plants are described by their business conditions and production volumes: Toyota, Nissan, Mitsubishi, Toyo Kogyo (Mazda), Honda, Isuzu, and Suzuki.

256. Treece, James B., David Woodruff and Karen Lowry Miller. "Japanese carmakers are coddling their U.S. kids." Business Week. (March 4, 1991): 21.

The impact of economic recession on the Japanese and U.S. auto sales is discussed. In most cases, Japanese carmakers cut back exports from Japan instead of curtailing the U.S. output. U.S. auto experts predict that the present situation could ignite a costly incentive war among the U.S. and Japanese automakers if the recession lingers or deepens.

257. Treece, James B. "Can Detroit hold its lead on safety?" Business Week. 3189 (November 26, 1990): 127-30.

U.S. automakers have been ahead of the Japanese in safety measures. Air bags, antilock brakes, and traction control systems are expected to become common in all cars in the 1990s. Both U.S. and Japanese automakers are pushing their newly designed models for more safety features while readjusting for less mileage gains.

258. Treece, James B. "Shaking up Detroit: how Japanese carmakers are beating the Big Three on their own turf." Business Week. 3119 (August 14, 1989): 74-80.

The Japanese invasion of the U.S. auto market represents a major threat to Detroit, especially for the Big three--General Motors, Ford, and Chrysler. While cost-cutting and low volumes of car sales continues, the businesses involved in transplants keep rising steadily. The United States needs to learn the long-range strategy used by Japanese automakers and also needs to improve the quality of its products and employee management systems.

259. "Two ways to change gear." Economist. 313 (December 23, 1989): 11.

U.S.-Japanese competition in the luxury car market is covered in this article.

260. "U.S. and Japan develop new action plan to increase U.S. auto parts sales to Japan." Business America. III.13 (July 2, 1990): 15-16.

United States and Japanese government officials have developed a new action plan to increase worldwide sales of U.S. automobile parts and components to Japanese automobile manufacturers. The plan will provide a framework to speed up the purchases of U.S. auto parts and components. It also acknowledges the need for U.S. parts suppliers to learn the design phases of Japanese motor vehicle and auto parts development.

261. United States. Congress. Senate. Committee on Small Business. Subcommittee on Innovation, Technology, and Productivity. United States/Japan auto parts trade: hearing before the Subcommittee on Innovation, Technology, and Productivity of the Committee on Small

Business, United States Senate, One Hundred First
Congress, first [i.e. second] session ... April 20, 1990.
Washington, DC: U.S. Government Printing Office, 1990.

The auto parts trade deficit between the United States
and Japan has grown steadily almost five-fold since 1980.
It now accounts for over 10% of the total U.S.-Japanese
trade imbalance. At a time when Japanese auto parts were
allowed to enter this country, American suppliers have
less than a 1% share of the market for auto parts in
Japan. This document, especially targeted at small- and
medium-sized firms in the United States that face
barriers in trying to sell to Japanese companies,
discusses the trade problem in auto parts between the
United States and Japan, analyzes the Japanese trade
system, and evaluates U.S. Government trade regulations,
such as Section 310 of the Trade Act of 1974, known as
Super 301, concerning the establishment of a legal
structure that the U.S. Administration can utilize to
seek a fundamental change in the trading relationship
between the United States and Japan in auto parts.

262. United States. Dept. of Commerce Economic Affairs. Office
of Business Analysis. The U.S. motor vehicle and
equipment industry since 1958. Washington, DC: U.S.
Dept. of Commerce, 1985.

This volume contains several joint reports prepared by
the Industrial Analysis and Productivity Research Program
(IAPR) of the Office of Business Analysis. It contains
a comprehensive analysis of the U.S. motor industry,
current trends in consumption, production, design,
product development, and import penetration, industry
performance and labor management, with statistics from
the period 1958 to 1980.

263. United States. General Accounting Office. Report to
Congressional Requesters. Foreign investment: growing
Japanese presence in the U.S. auto industry. Washington,
DC: U.S. Government Printing Office, 1988.

This report addresses the concerns of foreign investors
in the United States auto sector; the market share for
U.S. companies; and industry overcapacity. The job
impact of the U.S. autoworkers and the increasing U.S.
presence of Japanese assembly plant workers are the
primary topics in this report. Studies on estimated net
job loss were conducted by the United Auto Workers (UAW)
and General Accounting Office.

264. "Universal motors takes over: the new 'Big Three' will be
Europe, Japan, and the U.S." World Press Review. 36.1
(January 1989): 36-37.

A growing trend toward a global auto industry is the
cooperation between companies of different origins
through joint ventures or close relations. Reducing
costs, superior product development, and better consumer
services become crucial in these days. An overview of

the auto manufacturing industry in Japan, Europe, and the United States is included.

265. Volpato, Giuseppe. "The automobile industry in transition: product market changes and firm strategies in the 1970s and 1980s." In The automobile industry and its workers: between Fordism and flexibility. New York, NY: St. Martin's Press, 1987, pp. 193-223.

Between 1970 and 1980, the car industry went through a very complex process of transition. This chapter analyzes the car industry in Japan, the United States, and Europe during 1970-1980 from demand, competition, the internationalization of markets, automation, auto components industry, and management points of view.

266. Wickens, Barbara. "Driving upscale." Maclean's. 103.42 (October 15, 1990): 52-54.

Japanese automakers are releasing upscale luxury models which are designed to compete with traditional luxury car makers like Cadillac, BMW and Mercedes-Benz. Details of luxury car models offered by American and Japanese makers are described.

267. Wong, David. "The U.S. auto industry in the 1990s." Business Review. (July/August 1990): 11-20.

U.S. auto sales in 1990s shows a gradual decline. Auto experts attribute most of this to a combination of slower economic growth, more restrictive terms of auto loans, and the sales boom which lasts for a sustained period of time. Once all of these factors fade out, auto sales should rebound. Japanese automakers are aggressively making inroads into the United States. The market competition between these two countries is likely to heat up. It is expected that the U.S. auto industry in the 1990s will face more competitive situations between U.S. and Japanese automakers in terms of market shares, production volume, quality control and labor-management issues.

268. Woodruff, David. "The Japanese borrow Detroit's favorite ploy: rebates." Business Week. (June 17, 1991): 34.

U.S. and Japanese competition in the American auto market is discussed. Detroit's Big Three suffered a severe loss of $2.4 billion in the first quarter of 1991 and are likely to loose $1.1 billion in the second. In the meantime, Japan's market share continues to grow. The latest market strategy is offering rebates and cut-rate leases to dealers or buyers. Japan is also holding on to younger auto buyers by selling them what they desire. This situation is quite disadvantageous for Detroit's automakers. They should fight even harder in order to win the market share back again.

269. Woodruff, David. "A new era for auto quality." Business Week. 3184 (October 22, 1990): 84-96.

Discusses the quality control issue for both Japanese and
American cars. The new concept defined by the Japanese
automakers is to make cars that are not only reliable but
also fascinate, bewitch, and delight. Detroit is trying
to catch up with the quality issue. The Big Three lead
on features such as auto safety and comfort, while the
Japanese emphasize fuel efficiency and compact designs.
Both sides are now redefining their goals to produce
better quality, fascinating designs for cars to fit
diversified customers' needs.

270. Woodruff, David.   "Big bets on a little engine."
     Business Week. (January 15, 1990): 81-83.

     American, Japanese, and European auto makers are
     competing vigorously to complete a new generation of
     two-stroke engines. The attraction of two-strokes is
     that their simplicity, small size, and efficiency could
     save manufacturers $200 to $400 per unit. The engines
     have about 200 fewer components than a conventional
     engine, produce about 50% more power, and amount to 20%
     more fuel savings compared to a four-stroke engine. The
     Orbital Engine Co. in Australia pioneered the two-stroke
     engine design on automobiles. Toyota, Fuji, and Chrysler
     followed suit. However, stricter emission standards in
     the revised Clean Air Act may slow the introduction of
     the engines into the market.

271. Woodruff, David.   "Does Detroit have the oomph for the
     hills ahead?" Business Week. 3134 (November 20, 1989):
     83A, C.

     Tighter auto pollution control and fuel-efficiency
     standards have had great impact on American as well as
     Japanese cars. Since the Japanese react to change faster
     than Detroit, the new rules are even more worrisome to
     the U.S. auto companies. Tougher pollution and fuel
     standards could help sell more Japanese cars, increasing
     their U.S. market shares. In order to meet the Japanese
     challenge, the Big Three are all developing new models
     and engines to meet increasing mileage standards,
     fuel-efficiency, and pollution control rules.

272. Work, Clemens P.   "Detroit's drive for the fast lane."
     U.S. News & World Report. 108 (January 22, 1990): 40-41.

     An analysis of the status of the U.S. and Japanese
     automobile industry in the 1990s from the American
     industrial market point of view is offered. The
     technological comparison and business competition between
     Detroit's Big Three and the three Japanese auto giants
     which opened transplants in America, i.e. Honda, Toyota,
     and Nissan, are analyzed in this paper as well.

3

Japanese Transplants in the United States

273. Alster, Norm. "Unlevel playing field." <u>Forbes</u>. 143.13
     (June 26, 1989): 53-58.

     The growing number of transplanted Japanese suppliers and
     the close ties of Japanese automakers to their domestic
     component suppliers are the two major reasons for their
     penetration and acceleration in the U.S. auto market.
     The tough competition has forced many U.S. companies to
     raise their standards and cut their costs. One survival
     technique suggested by the author is to have small U.S.
     suppliers enter into joint ventures with Japanese firms.
     Americans should watch for the quality of products while
     Japanese should have a truly open attitude toward a
     harmonious industrial relationship between the two
     nations.

274. Armstrong, Larry. "So far, Nissan's catch-up plan hasn't
     caught on." <u>Business Week</u>. 3178 (September 17, 1990):
     59-66.

     1990 was supposed to be a transition year for Nissan.
     The company switched its market focus from entry level
     buyers to the upscale customers. However, car sales in
     the U.S. were not so good in 1990. They fell 13% during
     the first half of the year. Nissan blamed the drop on
     its decision to shift emphasis from its entry-level
     Sentra to the larger Stanza, but sales of other models
     have fallen as well. The company recruited Thomas D.
     Mignanelli to restructure the U.S. operations. He
     undertook new personnel arrangements and financial
     reorganization. A brand new Stanza, Nissan's first car
     to be designed, engineered, and produced in America, is
     due in 1992.

275. Berry, Bryan H. "An American workforce produces Japanese
     quality." <u>Iron Age</u>. 229.14 (July 18, 1986): 44-50.

Nissan Motor Manufacturing Corp. started its U.S.
operation by first producing trucks at its plant located
in Smyrna, Tennessee, in 1983. By the end of 1986, the
plant began producing Sentra cars in the United States.
Most employees at Smyrna are local people. The plant
tries to build cars and trucks as good as or better than
those produced at its plant in Japan. Quality control,
plant management, and job rotation are three major
focuses at Nissan. The company prefers not to join the
United Auto Workers Union for fear of less job security
and restrictions on personal involvement in
decision-making processes.

276. Berry, Bryan H. "Nissan was first." Iron Age. 229.10
     (May 16, 1986): 32-35.

     Compares Nissan Motor Co. Ltd. with Honda of America
     Manufacturing Inc.(HAM) in terms of their market
     strategies, management techniques, personnel
     arrangements, and labor unions.

277. Berry, Bryan H. "Inside Honda's plant in Marysville,
     Ohio." Iron Age. 226.17 (June 15, 1983): 26-27.

     Honda of America Manufacturing Inc., the first U.S. plant
     built by Japanese automakers, began its operation in
     September 1979, in Marysville, Ohio. After meeting high
     quality standards for its motorcycle production, Honda
     invested heavily in producing automobiles in the United
     States. Honda Accord was the company's first car built
     in the U.S. The company's success is attributed to the
     harmonious relationship between its workers and unions,
     guaranteed job security, mutual respect, and low
     absenteeism.

278. Bryan, Michael F. and Michael W. Dvorak. "American
     automobile manufacturing: it's turning Japanese."
     Economic Commentary. (March 1, 1986): 1-4.

     The sharp declines in the value of the dollar relative to
     the yen and the lucrative U.S. market are two major
     reasons for the relocation of Japanese automakers in the
     United States. Although they may lose some production
     advantages, they make efforts to maintain good labor
     relations and production management with their local
     workers. Seven assembly plants have been established in
     America so far. It is estimated that these Japanese
     plants will be able to produce around 1.4 million units
     annually by 1989, representing an investment valued more
     than $3.5 billion.

279. Corrigan, Richard. "Japan's third wave." National
     Journal. 17.16 (April 20, 1985): 840-47.

     Japan's penetration of the U.S. auto market can be
     divided into three phases. First, the Japanese exported
     their cars to the U.S., and then followed with the
     establishment of U.S. assembly plants. The auto parts
     suppliers represent a third wave of Japan's entrance into

the American auto market. Most auto parts companies were
established in Michigan. The incentive for this move is
that the Japanese cannot retain its U.S. market share
under voluntary export restrictions unless they bring
their operations to the U.S.

280. Dutton, Barbara.   "Anatomy of a joint venture."
     Manufacturing Systems. 7.6 (June 1989): 18-22.

     Diamond-Star Motors (DSM), the result of a joint
     collaboration between Chrysler Motors Corp. and
     Mitsubishi Motors Corp., was established in Normal,
     Illinois and opened for production in September of 1988.
     The joint venture provides an opportunity for both sides
     to learn from each other's technology, manufacturing, and
     managerial techniques. This article presents a detailed
     analysis of the DSM facility, including the firm's
     technological cooperation, labor management, personnel
     coordination,   employee   training,   and
     manufacturer-supplier relationships. The primary goal of
     DSM is to merge the existing technologies and
     capabilities of Chrysler and Mitsubishi into one better
     corporation.

281. Edid, Maralyn. "Why Mazda is settling in the heart of
     union territory." Business Week. 2991 (September 9,
     1985): 94-95.

     In November 1984, Mazda Motor Corp. announced its plan to
     build a $450 million automobile plant in the heavily
     unionized state of Michigan. Mazda expects to boost its
     market share based on the cars produced in Flat Rock,
     Michigan as well as help ease trade frictions between the
     U.S. and Japan. Mazda chose Michigan for its favorable
     location, transportation facilities, and the state's $120
     million in financial and other incentives.

282. Hochi, Shozo. "Japanese auto companies: at home in
     America." Business Japan. 31.4 (April 1986): 24-29.

     This article reflects the personal experiences of the
     author on his visits to the several Japanese auto
     manufacturers operating in the United States: Honda of
     America Manufacturing Inc. (HAM), Nissan Motor
     Manufacturing Corp. (NMMC), and the New United Motor
     Manufacturing Inc. (NUMMI). It describes his observation
     on the reaction of U.S. labor to the Japanese managerial
     and production systems adopted by these automakers. The
     article gives a detailed description of each assembly
     plant, including the following major features: historical
     development, labor management, corporate culture,
     production schedules, and teamwork concept.

283. Holusha, John. "Mixing cultures on the assembly line."
     New York Times. (June 5, 1988): C1, C8.

     The emerging trend of Japanese auto-manufacturing in the
     United States is transforming the U.S. automobile
     industry today. The joint ventures and assembly line

operations help to transform the way the domestic
industry operates, changing the nature of global
competition, and bringing new types of Japanese
management to the U.S. factories. This article features
a description of these U.S.-Japanese joint ventures, the
impact on the domestic industry of business competition
between the two.

284. Inaba, Yu. "The final battle: Japan takes on the U.S.
     luxury car market." Tokyo Business Today. 58.2
     (February 1990): 26-31.

Japanese automakers launched luxury cars in the U.S.
since 1989. The first one, Toyota's Lexus 400, began
being marketed in the U.S in April 1989, and sold 3,439
units during its first month of sale. Nissan sold 400
units of its Infiniti Q45 during its first two days on
sale in November of that same year. Along with this
sales thrust in the U.S. luxury car market, Japanese auto
plants are also approaching full-scale local production
in America. Honda of America Manufacturing Inc. (HAM),
Nissan Motor Manufacturing Corp. (NMMC), and New United
Motor Manufacturing Inc. (NUMMI), a joint venture between
Toyota Motor and GM, all adopted Japanese-style
management methods and have established close ties with
the local community.

285. Kenney, Martin and Richard Florida. "How Japanese
     industry is rebuilding the rust belt." Technology
     Review. 94 (February/March 1991): 24-33.

The new wave of Japanese transplantation in the American
heartland has had a severe impact on the U.S. automobile
industry. The unique infrastructure of the Japanese
production organization, corporate strategy and close
coordination among its workers has made the country so
successful in setting up plants and doing business in the
United States that Detroit's Big Three can hardly
compete. This article analyzes Japanese corporate
management, production organization and auto assembly.
It also compares current U.S. economic status with the
Japanese transplant businesses and offers some
perspectives in lieu of Japanese competition.

286. Kraar, Louis. "Japan's gung-ho U.S. car plants."
     Fortune. 119.3 (January 30, 1989): 98-108.

This report includes an analysis and review of the six
Japanese transplants: Mazda, Subaru-Isuzu, Diamond-Star
(Chrysler and Mitsubishi joint ventures), Honda, Toyota,
and Nissan. These plants have created over 15,000
assembly jobs in the United States. The impact of these
plants on their American workers as well as all U.S.
automobile factories is tremendous. Auto production and
assembly line operations, social lives and
inter-relationships of Japanese and U.S. workers, effects
of plants on local residents and municipalities are all
fully described in this article.

287. LeCerf, Barry H. and Bryan H. Berry.   "Nissan's truck
     plant: people and robots under one roof."   Iron Age.
     225.26 (September 15, 1982): 29-33.

     Nissan's truck plant in Smyrna, Tennessee is the most
     automated truck plant in the world. It assembles 156,000
     trucks per year and can handle up to 240,000 with extra
     machinery.   Robots will provide Nissan with the most
     advanced   technology   in   the   automobile   industry.
     Automated system control and systematic personnel
     management are two significant assets of the company.

288. Levin, Doron P. "Honda to reduce output at auto plants
     in Ohio." New York Times. (July 8, 1992): D7.

     Due to the sluggish economy in the United States and
     strong competition from the Big Three automakers, Honda
     of America Manufacturing Inc. plans to cut back
     production at its assembly plants in Marysville and East
     Liberty, Ohio.   Moreover, Honda's Accord, the nation's
     best-selling model since 1989, has suffered slower sales
     in 1992, due to strong sales of Ford's Taurus.   Honda
     plans to lower its production by reducing the speed of
     assembly lines at its two Ohio plants, and by spending
     some half-days on training workers instead of laying them
     off.

289. Mankin, Eric D. and Robert B. Reich.   "Joint ventures
     with Japan give away our future."   Harvard Business
     Review. (March/April 1986): 78-86.

     The impact of Japanese transplants on the American
     economy, employment, labor market, and technology
     transfer are described.   The Japanese strategy is to
     avoid U.S. trade barriers by investing in the United
     States and allying with U.S. companies. These companies
     often view a joint venture with a Japanese company as an
     inexpensive way to enter a potentially lucrative market
     and to produce low-cost and high-quality products.
     Increased competition in the domestic market and the
     continued declining sales of the Big Three have all
     contributed to the effects of growing Japanese pressure
     in the U.S. market.   This paper addresses several
     problems which U.S. industry faces at the present time,
     and describes the prospects of U.S. industries in the
     future.

290. Matumoto, Yutaka.   "Future car competition centers on
     America." Business Japan. 30.9 (September 1985): 22-23.

     The overseas production of major Japanese transplants in
     the U.S. is discussed. Japanese automakers have depended
     heavily on exports to the U.S. for many years. Since the
     voluntary export restrictions went into effect in 1985,
     many Japanese auto companies started building their
     plants in the U.S. in order to increase local production
     volumes.   The fierce competition in the American auto
     market will be played by leading Japanese automakers.

291. Newman, Richard G. and K. Anthony Rhee. "Midwest auto transplants: Japanese investment strategies and policies." Business Horizons. 33.2 (March/April 1990): 63-69.

This paper includes an overview of Japanese transplants in the Midwest. There are 90% of Japanese automotive businesses in the Midwest, including the states of Illinois (Diamond-Star), Indiana (Subaru-Isuzu), Kentucky (Toyota), Michigan (Mazda), Ohio (Honda), and Tennessee (Nissan). This article discusses issues from Japanese perspective about the factors that influence their decision to locate a transplant site in the United States; the economic development of the Midwest and states involvement in new plants; the analysis of common patterns for plants selections, and the regional impact on economic policy, labor force, management style and tax incentives.

292. Newman, Richard G. "The second wave arrives: Japanese strategy in the U.S. auto parts market." Business Horizons. 33.4 (July/August 1990): 24-30.

The invasion of Japanese manufacturers and auto suppliers has created a tremendous impact on the U.S. auto parts market. This article details how the Japanese parts industry invested in the "auto alley", the individual state's contributions involved with the transplants' business, the second phase of Japanese migration in the United States during the 1980s, and the major factors played by the Japanese along with their principle of "keiretsu". The final part of this article covers a comparative study of Japanese transplants and the Big Three, discusses the problems faced by U.S. auto industry, and provides possible solutions for the U.S. auto market in the future.

293. Nissan in Tennessee. Smyrna, TN: Nissan Motor Manufacturing Corporation U.S.A., 1983.

This book was written to commemorate Nissan Motor Company's building of its first U.S. automotive assembly plant in Smyrna, Tennessee. The announcement was made on October 30, 1980 by officials in Dearborn, Michigan. It was estimated that the cost would be at least $300 million, turning out 10,000 small pickup trucks a month, and creating 2,200 jobs for local residents. Throughout this book, we can see the real impact of a foreign automobile industry prospering in a small town like Smyrna, Tennessee. It is also a symbol of success for Japanese automotive investment in the United States.

294. Nobuto, Osamu. "Mazda in America." In The auto industry ahead : who's driving?. Arnesen, Peter J., ed. Ann Arbor, MI: Center for Japanese Studies, The University of Michigan, 1989, pp. 11-18.

Osamu Nobuto, the President of Mazda Motor Manufacturing Corporation (MMUC), describes the role the company played

in the American auto market, especially Mazda's
relationship with its U.S. parts suppliers. The author
offers his view on the operation and projection of the
company, the difficulties and differences between the
American and Japanese suppliers, and the future goals and
expectations of the company.

295. Pendleton, Jennifer.   "Will Americans buy an 'Ohio
     Honda'?" Advertising Age.   54.36 (August 29, 1983):
     M4-M5, M26.

     Nissan Motor Co. Ltd. and Honda Motor Co. Ltd., the
     second and third largest U.S. automobile importers,
     respectively, have opened up American plants.   Due to
     import protectionism, Japanese automakers are forced to
     set up U.S. operations.   Vehicles produced here are not
     subject to the voluntary restraint agreement. While both
     companies want to invest their money in U.S. business,
     they must deal with the competitive domestic products
     marked with the "Made in America" label.

296. Phalon, Richard.   "It's tough, but it isn't doomsday."
     Forbes.   139.10 (May 4, 1987): 53-55.

     This article describes the beneficial status of the
     Subaru of America, Inc. in the U.S. automobile market.
     Its medium-priced front- and four-wheel-drive Japanese
     imports have become almost the models for their admirers.
     Even though the competition is tough in the U.S. auto
     market due to the swift incursion of South Korean's
     Hyundai Excel and the rising yen which has priced many
     imports at prices well over comparable American models.
     In partnership with Isuzu Motors, Fuji Heavy Industries
     is building a plant in Lafayette, Indiana, to increase
     production and create a currency hedge for Subaru.

297. Raia, Ernest.   "The Americanization of Honda."
     Purchasing.   108.5 (March 22, 1990): 50-57.

     Records the market strategy and industrial management of
     the Honda of America in Marysville, Ohio. Honda Accord,
     currently the most popular car in the United States, is
     the company's first car that used mostly domestic content
     of auto materials.   Since then, Honda's policy has been
     given priority to nearby sources of production materials
     that can meet the company's quality, cost, and
     "just-in-time" delivery standards.   Honda's plan is to
     establish a self-sufficient manufacturing system in North
     America by the early 1990s.

298. Rehder, Robert R.   "Japanese transplants: in search of a
     balanced and broader perspective." Columbia Journal of
     World Business.   24.4 (Winter 1989): 17-28.

     The growing number of Japanese transplants in America
     threaten Detroit's auto business.   In spite of the
     overcapacity problem, Japanese auto production continues
     to expand, the quality of their products keeps refining,
     and their market shares continue to grow.   The American

auto industry is trying to adopt Japanese management techniques, and labor relations systems. The overall organizational structure, human resource management, job security system, and union versus non-union approaches between the U.S. and Japanese auto plants are analyzed.

299. Rehder, Robert R. "Japanese transplants: a new model for Detroit." Business Horizons. 31.1 (Jan./Feb. 1988): 52-61.

The Japanese impact on the U.S. automobile industry is discussed. Some of the major joint ventures which have been formed include General Motors and Toyota, Chrysler and Mitsubishi, and Ford and Mazda. These operations have developed real competitive power, due to the high cooperation of labor and management, and product quality, as well as their competitive prices on the U.S. market. The "kaizen" culture encourages team members to seek constant improvement for the company and products. The "jidoka" theory aims at establishing harmonious relationships between people and machines in order to build in quality. These management and organization models are now fully recognized by the Big Three. However, it is not easy for U.S. auto plants to adopt these strategies due to the complexities of cultural and labor-management differences.

300. Rice, Faye. "America's new no. 4 automaker--Honda." Fortune. 112.9 (October 28, 1985): 30-33.

This article details the role of Honda in the U.S. auto market. As the fourth largest producer, Honda has made enormous progress in the three years since it began U.S. production in 1979. Profit for the year ending February 1986 was $665 million, and $125 million of the gain came from U.S.-made Honda autos. Corporate performance and new product lines are discussed.

301. Rubenstein, James M. "The impact of Japanese investment in the United States." In Restructuring the global automobile industry. Law, Christopher, ed. London ; New York, NY: Routledge, 1991, pp. 114-42.

The impact of Japanese investment in the United States is examined. There are four major elements discussed in this chapter: 1) the impact on the U.S. motor vehicle market, 2) the impact on production strategies adopted by U.S. firms, 3) the impact on the location of motor vehicle plants in the U.S., and 4) the impact on local communities where Japanese plants are located.

302. Senia, Al. "Japanese automaking lands in America: what it means to U.S. suppliers." Production. 98.5 (November 1986): 42-49.

Analyzes three automobile transplants in the United States which are viewed as the wave of the future for the Japanese automobile industry. They are Nissan Motor Co. Ltd. in Tennessee, Honda of America Manufacturing Inc. in

Ohio, and New United Motor Manufacturing Inc. in
California.

303. Shimada, Haruo. Industrial relations and "humanware": a
study of Japanese investment in automobile manufacturing
in the U.S. Cambridge, MA: MIT-Japan Science and
Technology Program, 1986.

The Japanese automobile industry has been operated with
remarkable production performance and highly cooperative
industrial relations. This book analyzes the Japanese
production system and addresses the technological
connection between the system itself and its human
resources. Four major issues are discussed in regard to
Japanese transplant operations in the United States:
technological development and the production system;
personnel training; work organization and its functions;
and industrial relations. In conclusion, the future
perspective of the Japanese investments and their mutual
learning and cooperation experiences with the U.S. auto
industry are detailed.

304. Stavro, Barry. "Made in the U.S.A." Forbes. 135.8
(April 22, 1985): 50-54.

Several Japanese automobile manufacturers have built
plants in America. These companies include: Honda,
Nissan, and Toyota. Mazda will begin production in 1987
and Mitsubishi is seeking sites. It is expected that
within ten to twenty years these plants will be producing
major components and even designing cars for the local
market. This increased competition will eventually
change the whole structure of the global auto market.
There are three major factors to explain this: 1) U.S.
competition will be intensified while these Japanese
companies are expanding their U.S. operations; 2) Not
only auto manufacturers but also auto suppliers are
building their plants in the U.S.; and 3) The U.S. auto
import restrictions do not pose any threat to the
Japanese auto producers. Rather, they change their
production strategy and start building their operations
in the U.S.

305. Thompson, James R. "The Toyota decision." Economic
Development Review. 7.4 (Fall 1989): 21-23.

Toyota Motor Corp. built its $800 million auto plant in
Georgetown, Kentucky on December 11, 1985. This article
discusses Toyota's decision-making process and describes
the nature of the incentive program offered by Kentucky
which attracted Toyota to build its plant there. Major
factors include: 1) the state's abundant resources, 2)
the fairest tax system in the United States, 3) the
central location, 4) a commitment to educational
advancement, and 5) an interstate highway system with a
major intersection near the area.

306. "U.S. wheels are popular abroad." Journal of Commerce
and Commercial. (August 30, 1990): 2C, 6C.

United States auto and truck exports will surpass 305,000 units in 1990, and about 450,000 units will be expected by 1995. However, many exported vehicles come from foreign automakers' U.S.-based plants. For example, Honda of America (HAM) exported 5,000 of its Accord in 1989 to Japan. HAM eventually expects to export 10% of its cars made in the U.S. plants back to Japan.

307. "Unveiling the global car." Economist. 306.7539 (February 27, 1988): 54-55.

Japanese investment in the U.S. automobile industry is examined. Honda is the leading Japanese auto company that built an assembly plant in America, others form joint ventures with the United States. Beyond investment in America, Japanese automakers have also expanded their markets to European countries.

308. "Why Japanese auto makers hesitate to go to the United States?" Oriental Economist. 48.80 (April 1980): 6-9.

This article discusses the reasons why Japanese automakers are somewhat hesitant to set up production facilities in the U.S. The attitudes of the U.S. car industry are part of the reason, and the economics of competing in the United States are another part. The Big Three auto executives present their views about the situation.

309. "You know who is flooring it again: Japanese carmakers step up capacity." Business Week. (October 9, 1989): 66.

This report shows how heavily Japanese carmakers increased their investments in the U.S. and European markets since the voluntary export restraints went into effect in 1981. The Japanese spend most of their money on developing more advanced products and fine-tuning design and manufacturing. Carmakers in the United States and Europe are now confronted with global competition from the Japanese auto market.

4

Joint Ventures

310. Campbell, Harrison S., Jr. "State and regional economic impact of Diamond-Star Motors." Economic Development Review. 7.3 (Summer 1989): 31-34.

The joint venture between Chrysler Corp. and Mitsubishi Motors Corp. began on October 7, 1985 in Bloomington, Illinois. The Diamond-Star Motors Corp. was thus established to produce 240,000 subcompact cars per year beginning in September 1988. This article provides an in-depth analysis of the potential economic effects of Diamond-Star at the regional, state, and multi-regional levels. A study was conducted to assess the impact of Diamond-Star on Illinois and its seven regions. The relationship between employment and income, and the importance of household spending in generating employment are two major concerns of this study.

311. Ephlin, Donald F. "Japanese labor relations: a view from organized labor." Journal of Labor Research. 11.3 (Summer 1990): 299-305.

Japanese labor and management relations are fully explained using NUMMI, the joint venture between General Motors and Toyota, as an example. NUMMI is a very successful operation. It represents typical labor and management coordination based on mutual trust and respect between Japanese and American workers. The United States can learn from Japan in areas such as labor productivity, job security, and comprehensive retirement and reward systems.

312. "Ford to invest $380 million in venture, a Michigan car plant built by Mazda." Wall Street Journal. (July 2, 1992): B3.

Ford Motor Co. broadened its alliances with Japan's Mazda Motor Corp. by injecting $380 million into their joint venture plant in Flat Rock, Michigan. The plant now operates as a 50-50 venture called Auto Alliance International Inc. Ford also increased its investment in Autorama, a joint venture with Mazda that distributes Ford vehicles in Japan.

313. Gardner, Mona J., Han Bin Kang and Dixie L. Mills. "Japan, USA: the impact of the Diamond Star Plant on the Bloomington-Normal economy and housing market." Illinois Business Review. 44.6 (December 1987): 7-10.

The impact of Diamond-Star Motors, a joint venture between Chrysler Corp. and Mitsubishi Motors Corp., on the local area, is discussed in this article. The authors analyze trends in housing values, employment by sector, income, population, and other variables to justify whether the projected economic benefits of the plant are being realized. The data are collected for the period from January 1982 through early 1987. It shows that the period following the new plant announcement was accompanied by a rise in the prices of single-family housing, employment rates, and commercial loans in the Bloomington-Normal area as opposed to adjacent areas.

314. Horovitz, Bruce. "How 'old Toyota' views the sibling rivalry." Industry Week. 217.2 (April 18, 1983): 47, 50-51.

The Toyota/General Motors joint venture will set up its operation in Fremont, California. The new cars produced by Toyota/GM will be sold through GM's Chevrolet Motor Division. Toyota/GM will compete with Toyota Motor Sales USA, the "old Toyota". Norman Lean, chief operating officer of the "old Toyota", views the joint-venture company as a competitor.

315. Inaba, Yu. "Nissan comes to the rescue of Fuji Heavy Industries." Tokyo Business Today. 58.4 (April 1990): 18-19.

While Japanese automakers were enjoying big profits on domestic sales, Fuji Heavy Industries, Ltd. was the only one that announced sales losses, both at home and abroad. The Subaru-Isuzu Automotive Inc., a joint venture between Fuji and Isuzu Motors Ltd., was poorly timed for the U.S. market and coincided with a drop in demand in America. The main problem is its poor sales network in both the U.S. and Japan. Yutaka Kume, Nissan's President, has offered help to Fuji. The cooperation between these two companies will result in strengthened ties in personnel and production. Both sides will benefit from it.

316. Kerwin, J. Eugene and J. Donald Shea. "Interruption poses a threat to joint overseas ventures." Risk Management. 36.10 (October 1989): 24-30.

This is a case study of Diamond-Star Motors, a joint

venture between Chrysler Motors Corp. and Mitsubishi
Motors Corp. which was built in early 1988 in Normal,
Illinois. The production equipment needed to operate the
plant was specifically designed and built in Japan.
Thus, the company was relying on a dependable supply of
products shipped from Japan by railway or by sea. The
condition caused huge business interruptions. This
article addresses the constant problems of Diamond-Star,
and analyzes these problems by proposing possible
solutions.

317. Laver, Ross. "Lessons of the Orient." Maclean's. (March
     30, 1992): 32-34.

Chrysler's "LH" project, to build its first family sedans
based on Japanese automakers' team approach, is designed
to lower cost by dramatically shortening the cars'
production cycles. The past joint collaboration with
Mitsubishi Motors, named Diamond-Star Motors in Normal,
Illinois allowed Chrysler to learn the team concept of
developing new vehicles. After Chrysler pulled out of
the joint venture in 1991, the company has applied many
of the lessons it learned from Mitsubishi to the LH
project. The cars are expected to go on sale in October
1993 with a sticker price ranging from $17,000 to
$30,000, depending on their variable features.

318. Lind, Nancy S. and Ann H. Elder. "Who pays? Who
     benefits? The case of the incentive package offered to
     the Diamond-Star automotive plant." Government Finance
     Review. 2.6 (December 1986): 19-23.

This is a financial analysis and review of the site
selection processes of Diamond-Star Motors in McLean
County, Illinois. The economic development effort that
brought the company to McLean County was a three-level
process that involved the state, local government
officials, and the corporate hierarchy of
Chrysler/Mitsubishi. This study involves an examination
of the negotiation process between these three levels and
an assessment of the distribution of the costs of the
incentive package offered to Diamond-Star Motors.

319. Phillips, Stephen. "When U.S. joint ventures with Japan
     go sour." Business Week. 3116 (July 24, 1989): 30-31.

The joint ventures between U.S. and Japan were not quite
smooth and successful. Underlying the failures are
problems of divergent management styles, inflated
expectation, disputes over quality and labor practices,
and in some cases, bad luck. More important, the two
sides often entered into such ventures with very
different agendas. Quality is another trouble spot. As
this article points out, despite many ups and downs, the
Japanese are still in the United States for the long run.
They realize that the pay-and-gain strategy takes time
and they are willing to do for profits in the future.

320. Plumb, Stephen E.   "Detroit invests in hands-off policies." Ward's Auto World. (March 1990): 87.

A joint venture between Chrysler and Lamborghini to build the Diablo super car caused the vice president of Chrysler Corp. to review their policies when dealing with teamwork.   More partnership efforts between Japan and other foreign automobile companies are discussed in this article.   In most cases, both sides benefitted either from financial support or from technological assistance.

321. Rapoport, Carla.   "Mazda's bold new global strategy." Fortune.   122.15 (December 17, 1990): 109-13.

This article describes Mazda's strategic alliances techniques.   The company depends mainly on its import, production, and sales agreements with Ford, as well as deals with other automakers.   Mazda's top officials predict that the future of the world auto industry belongs to those who form well-targeted alliances.   Auto buyers want cars tailored to their own widely differing tastes, and that smaller companies allied with other automakers will be best able to deliver.   Mazda plans to introduce four to six new cars in 1991 which will be expected to range from fancier sport models to higher performance sedans.

322. "Saving the auto industry from itself: will Japanese know-how do the trick?" Dollar & Sense.   (April 1987): 6-9.

The cooperative venture between Toyota and General Motors to build the New United Motor Manufacturing Inc. (NUMMI) plant in Fremont, California is discussed.   The role of the transplant and its impact on the U.S. market are analyzed.

323. Sawicki, Elizabeth A. Feasibility of Japanese management techniques in American manufacturing: the case of New United Motor Manufacturing Inc. (NUMMI). Thesis (B.S. Honors, Business Administration)--Bucknell University, 1991.

This thesis presents an analysis of Japanese management techniques as practiced at the New United Motor Manufacturing Inc. (NUMMI), a joint venture between General Motors and Toyota.   Most employees of NUMMI are former GM workers while top management and production processes are borrowed from the Toyota production system. The results of this case study show that Japanese management is extremely effective and American companies should consider implementation of the Japanese techniques to improve their productivity.

324. Schreffler, Roger.   "Fuji and Isuzu in search of direction: a time for change; Isuzu, looking to build its own image, is stepping out of the GM shadows." Chilton's Automotive Industries. (June 1989): 66-67.

This article describes the current joint-venture
situation between Isuzu and GM. Most of these joint
efforts includes financial and technical assistance in
areas such as R&D, design, and production of vehicles.
In recent years, the company has faced many problems such
as the decline of truck sales volume, which the company
blames on the drop in output on the strong yen, and
export restrictions. Further improvement is underway.
One area is the application of ceramics on auto parts.
In the past, diesel engines marked the identity of Isuzu,
in the future, ceramics could do the same thing.

325. Serizawa, Yoshio. "Planning for growth in a Japanese
    business." Long Range Planning. 22.2 (April 1989):
    20-26.

    Japan Automatic Transmission Co. Ltd. (JATCO) was founded
    in 1971 by Ford (50%), Nissan (25%), and Mazda (25%). In
    1981, when Ford withdrew from JATCO, sold all of its
    shares to Nissan and Mazda, the new shareholding ratio
    changed into: Nissan 65% and Mazda 35%. In this article,
    the author as the president and Chief Executive Officer
    of JATCO, outlines the development of the company's
    corporate motto, philosophy and vision, the basic
    management strategies that were developed, and their
    achievements. He discusses the management planning
    system, its characteristics and the process of the plan
    and operating system, and the problems and lessons to be
    learned for future development of the company.

326. Smith, Charles. "Two-car family: Subaru driven into arms
    of Nissan." Far Eastern Economic Review. 148.17 (April
    26, 1990): 62.

    Fuji Heavy Industries, the eighth passenger car maker in
    the United States and owner of the Subaru brand name, is
    likely to form a joint collaboration with Nissan Motor
    Co. Fuji's recent problems include operating losses for
    its 1989 fiscal year, plus the company's failure to
    respond to the sharp rise in the yen-dollar exchange
    between 1985 and 1988. Subaru has been running at a loss
    in the U.S. since 1988. If the company merged with
    Nissan's North American network and was provided with the
    full range of Nissan models to sell, Subaru could become
    profitable again. But whether these two companies will
    merge or not may depend on how domestic sales perform.

327. Smith, David C. "Ford and Mazda enhance a global
    partnership: small-car program bridges cultures and an
    ocean." Ward's Auto World. (March 1990): 78-79.

    This is one of the biggest examples of Ford participation
    in joint ventures between Ford and Mazda, the
    collaboration of producing CT20 models, a small compact
    car that could compete directly with Honda Civic, Nissan
    Sentra, Toyota Corolla and Tercel, and GM's Geo line.

328. Smith, Joel and William Childs. "Imported from America:
    cooperative labor relations at New United Motor

Manufacturing, Inc."   <u>Industrial Relations Law Journal</u>.
9.10 (1987): 70-81.

The New United Motor Manufacturing Inc. (NUMMI), a joint
GM/Toyota operation, was formed in 1983.   This article
discusses the labor relations of NUMMI with United Auto
Workers (UAW).   In a letter signed by NUMMI and the UAW,
NUMMI agreed to provide stable, long-term employment to
its workers, and in return, the union would provide job
security and benefits to support the workforce and work
together with NUMMI to solve any corporate problems.

329. Tanzen, Andrew.   "We want to be like Audi and BMW".
     <u>Forbes</u>.   137.13 (June 16, 1986): 114-16.

Subaru of America Inc. is the best performing U.S. auto
stock of the past decade.   It imports fully assembled
cars from Fuji Heavy Industries' plants in Japan,
collecting an average margin of $500 per car.
Fuji/Subaru today accounts for half of all
four-wheel-drive cars sold in the U.S.   It is the only
company to offer a four-wheel-drive option on all its
models.   Faced with problems caused by the declining yen
and with competition in the four-wheel-drive market, Fuji
plans to push Subaru's product upmarket and is
considering expansion into Southeast Asia.   Fuji's
president claims that the company's goal is to be more
like Audi and BMW.

330. Treece, James B. and Karen Lowry Miller.   "The partners:
     surprise! Ford and Mazda have built a strong team.
     Here's how."   <u>Business Week</u>.   3251 (February 10, 1992):
     102-07.

After nearly 13 years of joint cooperation, the
Ford-Mazda team still stands strong in the auto market
world.   The alliance was founded in 1979.   Each side
shares and exchanges its valuable expertise--Ford in
international marketing and Mazda in manufacturing and
product development.   A comprehensive overview of the
joint venture and auto operations of the Ford-Mazda team
is analyzed in this paper.

331. Treece, James B.   "How Ford and Mazda shared the driver's
     seat."   <u>Business Week</u>.   3151 (March 26, 1990): 94-95.

This article shows how Ford's best-selling Escort was
built under joint product development between Ford Motor
Company and Japan's Mazda Motor Corporation in 1983.
Within a five year period, Ford worked on the style of
body design while Mazda engineered the mechanics. Both
sides resolved or reached a compromise on disagreements
about material, design, parts, and priorities. The 1991
Escort was a big success, not only saving at least $1
billion on budget for Ford, but also performing better
than initially expected.   Ford's best gain may be
realizing how Mazda works and what it must do to compete.

332. Treece, James B.   "An uneasy alliance on the Wabash."
     Business Week.   3130 (October 23, 1989): 59.

     This article analyzes the joint-venture situation between
     Isuzu Motors Ltd. and Fuji Heavy Industries Ltd.   There
     has been a great deal of conflict and struggle between
     these two companies since they joined forces on October
     1989, in Lafayette, Indiana. Subaru-Isuzu Automotive Inc.
     (SIA) are two factories under one roof.   It is difficult
     for both sides to reconcile the two corporate cultures.
     The company has not made any further plans to expand its
     present auto capacity at this time.

333. Treece, James B.   "Will Detroit cut itself loose from
     'captive' imports?"   Business Week.   3122 (September 4,
     1989): 34.

     The slumping U.S. auto market and tightening fuel economy
     standards   are   forcing   the   American   carmakers   to
     reconsider their auto-selling strategy with the so-called
     captive imports.   For example, the imported Isuzu and
     Mitsubishis   were   sold   as   Chevys   and   Dodges,   the
     U.S.-built Toyota Corollas went for sale as   Geo
     Prizms/Chevy Novas.

334. Tsutsui, Mikio and Shota Ushio.   "Mitsubishi and
     Daimler-Benz start collaboration." Tokyo business Today.
     58.11 (November 1990): 8-9.

     Discusses the possibility of joint ventures between
     Daimler-Benz A.G. and four Mitsubishi members (Mitsubishi
     Motors Corp.,   Mitsubishi Corp.,   Mitsubishi Electric
     Corp., and Mitsubishi Heavy Industries Ltd.).   The two
     sides express their concern and expectations for the
     collaboration efforts.   Japanese industry people focus
     their attention on the pair's possible cooperation for
     aircraft and racket development.   Mitshbishi Motors Corp.
     is enthusiastic about the possibility of collaboration
     because Mercedes car sales will win a better image for
     the company.

335. Vasilash, Gary S.   "NUMMI: proving that cars can be built
     in California."   Production.   104.2 (February 1992):
     36-41.

     New United Motor Manufacturing Inc. (NUMMI) is a joint
     venture between General Motors and Toyota established in
     1984.   The plant, located in Fremont, California,
     produced about 205,000 vehicles in 1990 on Geo Prizms and
     Toyota Corollas.   The venture's success is attributed to
     its dedicated workforce, harmony between NUMMI and the
     UAW, quality of life for employees, mutual respect and
     trust among executives and workers, and production
     efficiency.

336. Wrubel, Robert.   "If you can't beat 'em..."   Financial
     World.   159.7 (April 3, 1990): 30-34.

     Ford Motor Co. in Detroit, Michigan spent around $2

billion to develop the 1991 Escort with its 25%-owned partner, Mazda. Mazda engineered the car, Ford designed it, and Ford and its U.S. suppliers had to build 80% of the car in the United States. There are major differences between the two companies, such as labor management, cultural diversification, and computerized engineering systems. The cost for developing the Escort was higher than originally estimated so that it will sell at a small loss. However, Ford felt that manufacturing high-volume cars at low cost and high quality were well worth it.

5

Managerial Methods and Labor-Management Relations

337. Bairstow, Jeffrey. "Automated automaking." High Technology. 6.8 (August 1986): 25-28.

Japanese automakers are exporting their techniques to develop automated assembly plants abroad. Numerically controlled machine tools and industrial robots are extensively automated and applied in assembly plants. Highly automated auto plants are starting to appear in Japan, such as Mazda's Hofu plant in Hiroshima, which produces some 20,000 autos per month. Nissan is the leader in applying robots to vehicle manufacture. There are 2,000 robots in operation at the company's 10 auto plants in Japan.

338. Campbell, John Creighton, ed. Entrepreneurship in a "mature industry". Ann Arbor,MI: Center for Japanese Studies, The University of Michigan, 1986.

This book includes papers presented at the fifth annual U.S.-Japan Automotive Industry Conference which was held in March 1985. A surge of entrepreneurial behavior, organizational and technological innovations in product, manufacturing, internal organization, and relationships with ancillary firms and suppliers are the immediate concerns of the Japanese automobile industry today. The discussions in these papers are concentrated on the problems and changes through the "entrepreneurship" idea in order to lead Japan to a new era in the automobile industry.

339. Ceppos, Rich. "The leaning of America." Car and Driver. 36.17 (June 1991): 17.

This article describes the concept of the Japanese lean production system which was initially introduced by the president of Toyota Motor Co., Mr. Eiji Toyoda, in the

early 1950s. Lean production covers every single detail
of the automaking business--product planning, design,
manufacturing, engineering, and distribution. After
nearly four decades of application, the system proves to
be a highly efficient model for the Japanese automobile
industry. American companies are now trying to come up
with a functional equivalent through lean-style
organization team and production management techniques.

340. Chrysler, Mack. "Labor shortage strikes Japan: younger
workers want more time off, shun factories." Ward's Auto
World. (April 1990): 36-37.

Labor shortage problems have stricken Japanese automakers
in recent years. At the moment, small- and medium-sized
companies are suffering the most and the construction
industry complains of being short 400,000 workers. The
solution is very hard to come by. Automakers are now
relying more and more on part-time and seasonal workers,
but they are hard to get and expensive. Another option
is to automate the factory on the production line by
introducing more robots to replace human labor. Either
in one way or another, the shift to more automation is
bound to put an even sharper edge on Japanese
competitiveness.

341. Cusumano, Michael A. "Manufacturing innovation: lessons
from the Japanese auto industry." Sloan Management
Review. 30.1 (Fall 1988): 29-39.

This paper summarizes some of the major findings from a
five-year study of the Japanese automobile industry at
Nissan and Toyota. The study describes the Japanese
innovations in production management and examines their
remarkable improvements in productivity and inventory
levels. There are three basic policies generally adopted
by the Japanese auto companies: "just-in-time"
manufacturing, temporary reduction of process complexity,
and vertical de-integration between component production
and final assembly.

342. Cusumano, Michael A. The Japanese automobile industry:
technology and management at Nissan and Toyota.
Cambridge, MA: Council on East Asian Studies, Harvard
University, 1985.

This book addresses the successful managerial techniques
applied by Nissan and Toyota. Nissan's small-car designs
and low-cost production techniques are the important
factors which contribute to its success. While for
Toyota, the mutual coordination between managers,
workers, suppliers, and geographical conditions perfected
a system to produce and sell a few more cars per worker
per year. This book includes detailed analyses of these
two companies, with major focuses on company origins,
technology transfer from trucks to cars in the postwar
era, manufacturing management and labor, market strategy,
production management, and quality control in
manufacturing and design.

343. Fischetti, Mark A.   "Banishing the necktie."   IEEE
     Spectrum. (October 1987): 50-52.

     This article describes Japanese management style using
     the New United Motor Manufacturing Inc., a joint venture
     between General Motors and Toyota Motor Corp. as an
     example. Compared with the American industrial planning
     and management, and the structure and relationship of
     United Auto Workers (UAW) union with its workers, the
     Japanese style of management includes the following good
     features: 1) mutual trust and respect between the company
     and its workers through guaranteed job security, and
     equally shared responsibility among workers; 2) team
     concept--the teamwork at NUMMI is its key to solve major
     problems and to eliminate wasteful production steps; 3)
     managing the unions; and 4) global flexibility between
     the two joint companies.

344. Florida, Richard and Martin Kenney.   "Transplanted
     organizations: the transfer of Japanese industrial
     organizations to the U.S." American Sociological Review.
     56 (June 1991): 381-98.

     The industrial organization of Japanese transplants in
     comparison with the Big Three automobile companies is the
     main focus of this research paper. Over one hundred
     personal interviews with Japanese and American executives
     were conducted with major emphasis on investment
     strategies, location, production and organization,
     suppliers relations, and inter-organizational linkages.
     This paper explores the relationship of organization and
     environment using Japanese automotive transplants as an
     example to support the case of organizations that are
     being transferred from a supportive to a foreign
     environment.

345. Foust, Dean, et al.   "The UAW vs. Japan: it's showdown
     time in Tennessee."   Business Week.   3116 (July 24,
     1989): 64-65.

     Discusses the confrontation of Nissan Motor's non-union
     status with its workers.   Currently, the United Auto
     Workers (UAW) union represents workers at only three of
     the seven Japanese transplants in the United States.
     Unions are struggling to maintain its bargaining leverage
     as Japanese autos capture a big portion of the U.S.
     market.

346. Gelsanliter, David.   Jump start: Japan comes to the
     heartland. New York, NY: Farrar, 1990.

     This book describes in detail how Honda, Nissan, and
     Toyota manage their companies on the American land, and
     whether the emergence of Japanese workers enable American
     automakers to recapture core values that many had
     believed lost: the work ethic, a sense of mutual
     respect, and the high demand for quality products. Other
     major discussions in this volume include: Japanese

management, marketing strategies, labor unions, and impact and reactions of local people to transplants.

347. Holusha, John. "Japan's productive car unions." New York Times. (March 30, 1983): D1, D19.

During the past two decades of rapid development, the Japanese automobile industry has established an international reputation for its high quality of products, efficient management strategies, lowest absentee rates, and organized labor relations. This article explores the close ties between the unions in Japan with automobile companies, Japanese social and cultural backgrounds in association with their harmonious labor relations, and the comparative study of U.S.-Japanese labor-management strategies.

348. Holusha, John. "Just-in-time system cuts Japan's auto costs." New York Times. (March 25, 1983): A1, A9.

The "just-in-time" system is one of the few unique features of the Japanese automobile industry, which is based mostly on technology imported from the United States and Europe. It was first applied by Toyota, and gradually spread over the entire Japanese auto industry. Due to the effects of the system, Japanese companies spend nearly $500 less per car than the American automakers. This paper describes in detail the basic features of JIT system, such as the auto companies' benefits on production cost, inventory control, mechanical failure adjustment, work flow, and the intimate relationship between workers and suppliers. The comparison between the U.S. versus Japanese way of automobile production is also fully explored.

349. Japan Management Association, ed. Kanban, just-in-time at Toyota: management at the workplace. Stamford, CT: Productivity Press, 1985.

This book explores the Toyota Company's secret of success. It discusses the issues of the manufacturing process, Toyota production system, "just-in-time" and automation system, as well as workplace control and the kanban system.

350. "Japan ready to take next leap in factory automation." Ward's Automotive International. (September, 1991): 1-12.

Japan's four biggest automakers (Toyota Motor, Mazda Motor, Nissan Motor, and Honda Motor) will implement automation techniques in their final assembly line operations in the next few years. Each one has its own automated plan and goal for projected sales. This report describes in detail the construction plans and automation skills implemented by these Japanese car manufacturers.

351. "Japan's U.S. plants go union: labor-relations methods
     that work in Japan are not easily transplanted."
     Business Week. (October 5, 1981): 70-72.

     The unionization of Japan's U.S. plants is crucial for
     U.S. and Japanese industries. There are a great number
     of Japanese plants in the U.S., with a workforce of about
     110,000 Americans. Some are beginning to unionize, and
     this poses problems to Japanese managers in some cases.
     Japanese labor-relations methods are not quite as easily
     adopted by the American employees. Low wage and high
     production standards can become issues.

352. Kamata, Satoshi. Japan in the passing lane: an insider's
     account of life in a Japanese auto factory. New York,
     NY: Pantheon Books, 1982.

     This book depicts the realities of seasonal workers in
     Toyota's assembly plants, dealing primarily with Japanese
     industry and labor between 1972-73. The impetus for this
     volume came in large part from Kamata's conversation with
     a friend who had been a seasonal worker for several years
     at Honda Manufacturing Plants. He told Kamata of the
     grim working conditions, the boredom, monotony, incessant
     work demands, and of the high turnover rate of both
     regular workers and lower management employees. Kamata
     stayed at Toyota for a half year's contract to experience
     the situation personally, and the diary he kept there
     forms the basis of this book.

353. Kawahito, Kiyoshi.   "Labor relations in the
     Japanese automobile and steel industries." Journal
     of Labor Research. 11.3 (Summer 1990): 231-37.

     Labor relations in the Japanese automobile and steel
     industries   enjoy   harmonious   and   progressive
     relationships, and both contribute significantly to
     quality and productivity growth. This article describes
     the features of Japanese labor relations in these two
     industries. The four major elements are: lifetime
     employment, the seniority system, enterprise unionism,
     and teamwork.   A comparative analysis of these two
     industries is also covered.

354. Keller, Maryann. "Where America beats Japan." World
     Monitor. 4.1 (January 1991): 22-25.

     Discusses the status and working environment of U.S. and
     Japanese autoworkers.   The article points out that
     Japan's autoworkers are not satisfied with their
     treatment when there is workplace democracy while
     autoworkers in the U.S. are.

355. Kendall, Richard M. "Safety management: Japanese-style."
     Occupational Hazards. 49.2 (February 1987): 48-51.

     To find out how Japanese management techniques affect the
     safety and health of workers at Japanese companies
     operating in the United States, two of the U.S. largest

Japanese plants were interviewed, Honda of America Manufacturing Inc., in Marysville, Ohio, and Nissan Motor Manufacturing Corp., in Smyrna, Tennessee. The results show that Japanese safety management is characterized by: 1) participation of the workforce in decision-making on health and safety matters; 2) efficient, flexible work teams in charge of their own jobs; 3) shallow management hierarchies; 4) "just-in-time" delivery of materials; 5) peer pressure to work safely; 6) the use of job rotation to alleviate boredom; and 7) a demonstrated interest by top management in safety on the line.

356. Koshiro, Kazutoshi. "Personnel planning, technological changes and outsourcing in the Japanese automobile industry." International Journal of Technology Management. Part 1, 2.2 (1987): 279-97; Part 2, 3.4 (1987): 473-99.

This article is comprised of two parts. Part one examines the labor market strategy of Japanese firms. It includes an analysis of three models of the "life-time employment" system and employment adjustment after the oil crisis in Japanese manufacturing, automobile, and automobile assemblers industries. A case study is presented of personnel planning in the Japanese automobile industry. Part two analyzes the impact of industrial robots on employment and industrial relations in the Japanese companies and the cases of outsourcing in the automobile industry.

357. "Lean machines: Japan's success as a carmaker can be copied by any producer willing to learn." Economist. 316.7673 (September 22, 1990): 16-17.

Japan's success in the automotive industry has been discussed and analyzed by numerous auto experts in this field. "Lean production," a system initially developed by Eiji Toyoda and Taiichi Ohno at Toyota factory is the main attribute of the nation's success in the global auto business. This article focuses on the discussion of lean production, also called "just-in-time," and the utilization of the system in Japanese, American, and European auto companies.

358. Marsh, Robert M. and Hiroshi Mannari. Modernization and the Japanese factory. Princeton, NJ: Princeton University Press, 1976.

This book is a comparative study of Japanese industrial firms and auto companies with three major points of discussion: technological modernization, the modernization of social organization, and organizational performance or effectiveness on variations among firms in Japan. Features an overall discussion of Japanese industry settings, technology and the division of labor, job performance and social integration of the employee into the company.

359. Maskery, Mary Ann. "Informality seeps into Japanese
     management: Nissan leads way in new approach."
     Automotive News. (January 22, 1990): 3.

     This article shows how Nissan led the way in a new
     approach for changes in management style by reducing the
     layers of authority, and calling top officials by name,
     instead of title. A change from a conservative system
     into a more open way needs time to react. Since Nissan
     started, Toyota and other Japanese auto companies also
     followed in order to build a simple, productive, and
     clear-cut system of decision-making. Particularly now
     with the globalization of the auto industry, the trend to
     adopt internationally common features is indeed necessary
     for building a successful company.

360. Milkman, Ruth. "The impact of foreign investment on U.S.
     industrial relations: the case of California's
     Japanese-owned plants." Economic and Industrial
     Democracy. 13.2 (May 1992): 151-82.

     This document discusses the impact of Japanese direct
     investment on American workers and organized labor. It
     includes research findings and survey results on
     Japanese-owned plants in California, describes the
     implications of these plants for American workers and
     labor unions in the auto-manufacturing sector, and
     analyzes the labor-management relationships among the
     mixed U.S.-Japanese workforce at these Californian
     factories.

361. Mito, Setsuo. The Honda book of management: a leadership
     philosophy for high industrial success. London ;
     Atlantic Highlands, NJ: Athlone Press, 1990.

     This book discusses the management system of the Honda
     Motor Co. (HMC) built up by Mr. Soichiro Honda and his
     associates and the light it sheds on the concepts and
     assumptions of the managerial role in Japan. The study
     concentrates on the leadership philosophy and how this
     permeates four crucial aspects of managerial and
     organizational behavior, which are: top management
     organization, business strategy, product development
     activities, and workteam improvement activities.

362. Monden, Yasuhiro. Toyota production system: practical
     approach to production management. [Norcross, GA]:
     Industrial Engineering and Management Press, Institute of
     Industrial Engineers, 1983.

     The Toyota production system is a technology of
     comprehensive production management with the major
     purpose of increasing productivity and reducing costs.
     The basic idea is to maintain a continuous flow of
     products in factories in order to adapt flexibly to
     demand changes. The realization of such production flow
     is called "just-in-time" production at Toyota, which
     means producing only necessary items in a necessary
     quantity at a necessary time. Mr. Taiichi Ohno, former

vice-president of Toyota Motor Corp., is the inventor and promotor of the Toyota production system. The implementation of the system has proven to be very successful in Japan, especially in the automotive industry.

363. Okayama, Reiko. "Industrial relations in the Japanese automobile industry, 1945-70: the case of Toyota." In The Automobile industry and its workers: between Fordism and flexibility. Steven Tolliday and Jonathan Zeith. New York: St. Martin's Press, 1987, pp. 168-89.

This article describes the development of Toyota, its industrial relations and labor-management techniques from 1945 to 1970, putting major emphasis on the company's market and technological conditions. The period is divided into three phases: 1945-50 describes the labor and management relationships in the period immediately after the war; the 1950s focuses on the technological innovations during this period and their impact on work; the 1960s examines the mass-production system and managerial techniques which promote the implementation of the workforce into the automobile market.

364. Pollack, Andrew. "Japan lures auto workers with 'dream factories.'" New York Times. (July 20, 1992): A1, D2.

With rising prosperity and high living standards, young Japanese people no longer favor monotonous, fast-paced and tiring assembly line work. As a result, companies like Nissan, Toyota and Mitsubishi are all trying to create "friendly" factories that will be more comfortable for workers and will at least improve the image of auto factory work.

365. Rehder, Robert R. "Japanese transplants: after the honeymoon." Business Horizons. (January-February 1990): 87-98.

Japanese transplant operations in the United States create a big threat to the U.S. auto market. The three joint ventures between GM-Toyota, Chrysler-Mitsubishi, and Ford-Mazda are all highly successful businesses and have had a strong impact on the American auto market. This article provides a comparative analysis of three major issues between these Japanese plants and the U. S. Big Three: organizational management, labor unions, and labor-management relations.

366. Shimokawa, Koichi. "Product and labour strategies in Japan." In The Automobile industry and its workers: between Fordism and flexibility. Steven Tolliday and Jonathan Zeitlin. New York, NY: St. Martin's Press, 1987, pp. 224-43.

This paper examines the major factors which resulted in the international competitiveness of the Japanese auto industry; analyzes the product strategy of their auto manufacturers; investigates their labor-management

strategies and auto unions during the implementation of
the "just-in-time" system, and records the effects of the
JIT system to the flexibility processes and to the
innovative design and technological enhancement in the
Japanese automobile industry.

367. Takezawa, Shin-ichi, et al. <u>Improvements in the quality
of working life in three Japanese industries</u>. Geneva,
Switzerland: International Labor Organization, 1982.

This report covers a study on the changing patterns of
the quality of working life in three major Japanese
industries. They are: the ship-building, electrical
machinery and automobile manufacturing industries.
Chapter four discusses the Japanese automobile industry.
This chapter analyzes the following major issues:
union-management relations among autoworkers; the overall
employee benefits and services; the education and
training provided by Isuzu Motors, Ltd., Toyota Motor,
Honda Motor Co., Ltd., and Nissan Motor Co., Ltd.;
relationships between workers and assembly line
operations; and industrial management and quality
control of the products. The book concludes with
suggestions and mechanisms to improve the collaboration
between employers and trade unions as the major
ingredient in the quality of working life in Japanese
industries.

368. Teresko, John. "Japan's best plants: lean, efficient,
flexible, and worker-friendly." <u>Industry Week</u>. 241.17
(September 7, 1992): 33-39.

Along with the growing automobile production, the
Japanese automobile industry shows serious labor-shortage
problems. The industry is now moving its direction to
cast changes among its workforce, the robot, and other
machinery. America's slowed economy also drastically
affects Japan's automobile marketing plans. Japan
started its catch-up plans in the late 1940s when the
Ministry of International Trade & Industry set the goal
of an internationally competitive industry. The Japanese
auto companies realized that the MITI plan would not
succeed based on existing production methods. Companies
started to implement major changes in their auto
factories. The most notable change is Taichi Ohno's
Toyota production system in the early 1960s. The system
allows a much more efficient use of manufacturing
resources which reduces dramatically the requisite time
and workforce as well as costs.

369. "Transition in the Japanese auto industry: the emergence
of systemofacture." In <u>Driving force: the global
restructuring of technology, labor, and investment in the
automobile and components industries</u>. Kurt Hoffman and
Raphael Kaplinsky. Boulder, CO: Westview Press, 1988,
pp. [113]-79.

The major focus of this chapter is the development in
Japan of production organization and process technology.

The author starts with a brief description of the scale of the Japanese competitive advantage in the auto industry; then he reviews those features of production organization and labor processes which make the Japanese system unique; next he shows how Japan's auto companies integrate computer-based control systems and automation into their production systems; distinctive features of the relationship between component-supplies and suppliers are described in section four; finally, the analysis of the factors which influence the component industry in Japan, and locational decisions of these firms and their operations are included in the last section.

370. Vasilash, Gary S. "Discovering Japan." Production. 103 (January 1991): 39-51.

Japan's manufacturing system has gained world recognition of its superior performance, high efficiency, and quality of operations. To gain a better understanding of what makes the Japanese such successful manufacturers, the author examines three auto giants in Japan: Honda, Mazda, and Toyota. Honda's production system focuses on assigning the right parts in the designated place at the designated time in the designated amount. Mazda's so-called "model-mix" production system means there is no dedicated line; rather, an assortment is processed on any given line. The "just-in-time" production system at Toyota emphasizes low inventory control to yield quality of products.

371. Verespej, Michael A. "Nissan isn't an accurate gauge." Industry Week. 328.16 (August 21, 1989): 55.

Relates the union movement at Nissan Motor Corp's Smyrna, Tennessee auto plant. In spite of an 18-month campaign involving more than 30 organizers, a vote of 1,611 to 722 again kept the United Auto Workers out of the Japanese auto plant in Tennessee. One possible reason for the union loss is the lack of a key rallying point at a plant where workers already made 37% more than other area workers. The Nissan vote cannot represent a typical union's win-and-lose campaign. It is predicted that the union has a 61% win rate in work units under 50 employees which accounts for 35% of the workforce in the plant.

372. Wickens, Peter. The road to Nissan: flexibility, quality, teamwork. London: MacMillan, 1987.

Japanese investment in the United Kingdom has been growing rapidly for the past several years. Some of the key factors involved with the UK government's large grants, tax incentives and almost free factory sites. This book describes in detail the Nissan/Japanese management techniques applied in Nissan Motor Manufacturing (UK) Ltd. as well as Continental Can Company (UK) Ltd. where the author has been actually involved in the daily working environment in these two companies. The book addresses the major characteristics of Japanese-style management, their lifetime employment

system, the quality consciousness team, and their highly
integrated labor-management connections through the
author's personal involvement with these two companies.

6

Government Trade Issues

373. Armstrong, Larry and Karen Lowry Miller. "Japan's sudden deceleration: is Detroit winning back share, or is Tokyo giving it up?" <u>Business Week</u>. (June 8, 1992): 26-27.

The market competition between the Japanese and U.S. automobile industry is described. With overall sales running 5% ahead in 1992, American automakers have won back 1.2% of the U.S. car and truck market, raising their share to 72.1%. In Japan, the only automaker that shows a meaningful increase is Toyota Motor Corp. The political pressure for the Japanese started with President Bush's visit in January 1992. Japan's Ministry of International Trade & Industry started pressing automakers to raise prices. Other alternatives include lengthening model cycles, and increasing working hours. On the long-term basis, Japanese companies plan to continue their move to sell more high-margin models. While for the Big Three, their gains will primarily depend on selling cheaper, low-margin products.

374. Arnesen, Peter J., ed. <u>The auto industry ahead: who's driving?</u>. Ann Arbor, MI: Center for Japanese Studies, The University of Michigan, 1989.

The Japanese automobile industry has dominated the world auto market for a decade. The trade imbalances between the U.S. and Japanese auto industries have grown incessantly since the 1980s. This severe competition poses a major threat for U.S. automobile producers. Several major issues in this book address the Japanese situation from the U.S. point of view. The President of the Mazda Motor Manufacturing Corp. describes the operation of his company and offers an insider's view of the role the Japanese manufacturers played in the American industry. The impact of Japanese transplants on the American local community is also presented.

375. "Auto export quotas: a blessing in disguise?" <u>Business</u>
     <u>Japan</u>. 31.5 (May 1986): 16-17.

     In order to lessen the trade imbalances between the
     United States and Japan, the Japanese Ministry of
     International Trade & Industry decided to extend the
     export quota in 1986. Major discussions in this article
     include: statistics of Japanese domestic and export
     sales, debates on export quotas, the impact of U.S.
     export quota limits on the Japanese auto business.

376. <u>The Automobile industry in transition: regulatory trends</u>
     <u>and trade developments, June 24-25, 1991</u>. Washington,
     D.C.: Paul, Weiss, Rifkind, Wharton & Garrison, 1991.

     This report discusses government regulations concerning
     future trends and trade developments of the automobile
     industry in Japan, Canada, and Mexico.

377. Awanohara, Susumu. "Super 301: the sequel, U.S. bill
     targets Japanese trade." <u>Far Eastern Economic Review</u>.
     155.21 (May 28, 1992): 49-50.

     Super 301, a trade bill introduced by the Democratic
     leaders of the U.S. House of Representatives, is intended
     to initiate several trade incentives against Japan. If
     the bill passed, it will include strict guidelines for
     the U.S. Trade Representative to identify, negotiate
     with, and retaliate against, foreign countries that
     engage in restrictive trade practices. The bill will
     also set out limits on the production and sales of
     Japanese cars in the U.S. through a bilateral voluntary
     restraint agreement.

378. Boroughs, Don L. "Detroit gets a free ride: with U.S.
     layoffs rising, Japan faces harsh auto quotas." <u>U.S.</u>
     <u>News & World Report</u>. 3.27 (December 30, 1991): 58.

     The growing automotive trade deficit between Japan and
     the United States has had a severe impact on the entire
     American auto market. With the U.S. unemployment rate
     rising, Congress plans to impose the most severe
     restrictions on sales of Japanese cars in the United
     States. The new quotas could force Americans to pay
     hundreds or thousands more for the price of an average
     Japanese car and for auto maintenance jobs.

379. Borrus, Amy. "Tokyo unveils this year's 'Buy American
     plan'." <u>Business Week</u>. 3141 (January 15, 1990): 38-39.

     In order to solve the problem of the U.S. trade
     imbalance, the Japanese government made a special plea
     to its automakers to buy U.S. parts and will speed up its
     import drives in 1990. This article describes the
     promotion plans made by the Japanese Ministry of
     International Trade & Industry (MITI), and analyzes the
     impact of the plan on the U.S. trade deficit and
     government policies for the year of 1990.

380. Bradsher, Keith. "Honda's nationality proves troublesome
     for free-trade pact." New York Times. (October 9,
     1992): A1, D2.

     The U.S. Customs Service ruled that Honda's Civics which
     were assembled and imported from Canada in 1989 and 1990,
     with engines supplied by Honda's American plant in Anna,
     Ohio, violated the American local content legislation,
     and thus owed $17 million in duties on cars.   Both
     America and Japan are in critical debate about the
     effective date of the North American Free Trade
     Agreement. Under the 1988 rules of the U.S.-Canada trade
     agreement, the engines and cars were considered to be
     Japanese--thus incurring a total of $17 million in
     duties. But the new agreement, announced on August 12,
     treats the cars as Canadian, free from import duties.
     The qualification of Honda Civics' North American content
     has become a major trade issue between these two
     countries.

381. Bradsher, Keith. "U.S. trade agency turns down car
     makers' complaint on Japan." New York Times. (June 25,
     1992): A1, D6.

     This report describes the United States International
     Trade Commission's (USITC) decision to deny the Big
     Three's complaint that the Japanese import of minivans
     would harm Detroit's business. The USITC's decision was
     also meant to prevent the Commerce Department from
     proposing further plans to impose tariffs on the imports.
     Although the Big Three are not satisfied with the
     decision, they believe that Congress will eventually
     provide import protection for them.

382. Byron, Christopher. "How Japan does it: the world's
     toughest competitor stirs a U.S. trade storm." Time. 117
     (March 30, 1981): 54-60.

     U.S.-Japanese trade relations in the 1980s are analyzed,
     including such key issues as Japanese auto imports, U.S.
     government import restrictions on Japanese vehicles, the
     slumping U.S. auto market, Japanese management and labor
     relations, and government-business relationships in the
     Japanese auto industry.

383. Calton, Jerry Merle.   The political economy of
     international automotive competition: a comparative and
     longitudinal study of governmental policy, developmental
     change, and shifting competitive advantage in the
     European and Japanese automobile industries.   Thesis
     (Ph.D.)--University of Washington, 1986.

     This dissertation analyzes the relationship between
     patterns of government industrial policy intervention and
     variations in competitive advantage in the Japanese and
     European auto industries through successive stages of
     development from their inception to the present.

384. Ceppos, Rich. "How that Ford became a foreign." Car and
     Driver. 36 (April 1991): 25.

     The debates on U.S. domestic content legislation and the
     federally mandated corporate average fuel economy (CAFE)
     standard are discussed.

385. Chipello, Christopher J. "Japan car-dealer system irks
     importers." Wall Street Journal. (July 22, 1991): Sec.
     A, 5E.

     Japan's auto-distribution system which carries exclusive
     brands with their own dealer networks has been a focal
     point in the U.S.-Japan trade debate. This article
     discusses the status of Japan's dealership networks and
     how it relates to solving the U.S.-Japanese trade
     imbalances. The views from U.S. auto officials are
     offered.

386. Cole, Robert E., ed. The American automobile industry:
     rebirth or requiem? Ann Arbor, MI: Center for Japanese
     Studies, the University of Michigan, 1984.

     The awareness of Japanese competition with the United
     States auto market is the main theme of the lectures
     presented in this book. It includes papers on the
     following: U.S. auto policy; development and future
     problems of the Japanese auto industry; national
     industrial policy; the revolution at Ford concerning
     quality control of the products; manufacturer-supplier
     relationships; automobile revitalization; Japanese
     automobile taxes; and currency misalignment of the U.S.
     dollar and Japanese yen.

387. Cole, Robert E., ed. Industry at the crossroads. Ann
     Arbor, MI: Center for Japanese Studies, the University of
     Michigan, 1982.

     Major issues discussed in this volume include: government
     regulation of automobile safety; GATT rules (an
     international agreement made by the government entitled
     the General Agreement on Tariffs and Trade);
     internationalization of the auto industry on product
     development, product sourcing, and product manufacturing;
     the need for local content legislation regarding
     autoworkers' compensation and benefits using Japanese
     success as a good example; an analysis of Japanese auto
     plants, unions, inventory systems, technology and
     automation, product quality, and work force management;
     the "just-in-time" system and its relevance for the U.S.
     auto industry.

388. Crandall, Robert W. Regulating the automobile.
     Washington, DC: The Brookings Institution, 1986.

     Government regulations on automobiles and the impact of
     these rules on the auto industry business are examined.
     Three regulatory programs which are subjects of
     controversy include: federal emission standards imposed

on 1968 model automobiles; the tightened federal emission standards by Congress in 1970; and fuel economy standards legislated by Congress in 1975 for all new cars produced after the 1978 model year. This book evaluates these regulatory measures and the overall concerns affecting the U.S. auto industry both domestically and overseas.

389. Cullison, A. E. "Japan won't extend U.S. auto sales limits." Journal of Commerce and Commercial. 357 (July 1, 1983): 1A, 5A.

Japan's self-imposed auto export restrictions and U.S. protectionism against Japanese auto exports are the major issues debated by Japan's Ministry of International Trade and Industry and the U.S. Government.

390. Daniels, Jeffrey R. The motor industry and the environment. London: The Economist Intelligence Unit, 1990.

A growing concern for the quality of the human environment has been a major issue in recent years, especially among the three main vehicle-producing regions of Japan, Western Europe, and North America. This report discusses the environmental concern of the motor industry, the government legislations that imposed tightening emission controls for passenger cars, and the impact on, and trends of, the future of the automobile industry.

391. Denzau, Arthur T. Made in America: the 1981 Japanese automobile cartel. St. Louis, MI: Washington University, Center for the Study of American Business, [1986].

Voluntary export restraint (VER) was first announced by the Reagan Administration on May 1, 1981. It was the result of negotiation between the governments of the United States and Japan concerning the arrangement of a specific import quota for Japanese motor vehicles. This study argues that instead of providing greater chances for the American automotive industry to grow, the VER created more benefits for Japanese automakers selling cars and trucks in the U.S. by transforming their technological skills through setting up transplants in America. Trade restrictions on a short-term basis are ineffective, and the global competition keeps growing. This book examines the effect of the auto VER on Japanese companies and on the U.S. auto market. The likely impact of the depreciation of the dollar versus the yen is also analyzed.

392. Duncan, William Chandler. U.S.-Japan automobile diplomacy: a study in economic confrontation. Cambridge, MA: Ballinger Publishing Co., 1973.

The American effort to persuade Japan to lower trade and capital barriers began in the mid-1960s. Since then, this liberalization movement has been the most important economic issue in Japan. With American pressure for, and

Japanese reluctance against "automobile liberalization",
this has been a very sensitive issue between these two
countries. This book describes in detail the automobile
negotiations between the two as well as the Japanese
reorganization of the automobile industry after the
ending of trade liberalization.

393. Farnsworth, Clyde H.   "U.S. says import relief is
     unlikely for Detroit." New York Times. (March 26,
     1991): D2.

     The Big Three have been putting pressure on the auto
     officials in Washington, D.C. Among them, Chrysler has
     been the most active of the three companies on import
     issues. While House officials responded that they are
     unlikely to ask Japan for further export restraints on
     automobiles, they could offer assistance via temporary
     easing of some regulatory requirements.

394. Flint, Jerry. "Diggin' in, a note of cheer in a gloomy
     year for Detroit: the Japanese are no longer gaining
     market share." Forbes. 147 (March 18, 1991): 83.

     This report offers the market analysis of U.S. and
     Japanese vehicle sales in 1990 and 1991.   In 1990,
     Detroit's Big Three took 66% of the U.S. car sales. This
     year Detroit has slightly gained 2% more. The Japanese
     auto sector has taken 27.1% and 29.1% U.S. auto market
     sales in 1990 and 1991, separately. Although Japan made
     gains in the U.S. auto market, especially in the mid-size
     and upscale models, their operating profits may fall in
     spite of rising sales because of yen fluctuation. This
     situation seems to be a good sign for Detroit to compete
     with the Japanese and to catch up with the U.S. auto
     market again.

395. Fujigane, Yasuo.   "U.S., Japan: new quest for
     partnership." Tokyo Business Today. (January 1992):
     14-20.

     After President George Bush's visit to Japan,
     U.S.-Japanese trade relations became a hot debate and
     discussion on the news and in public. This analysis of
     the   U.S.   and   Japanese   economic   and   industrial
     interactions regarding automobiles and auto parts trades,
     discusses U.S. government legislations, local content
     laws, imports and exports with the goal of improving the
     U.S.-Japanese trade imbalances in the near future.

396. "General alarm: America's car makers."   Economist.
     321.7738 (December 21, 1991): 80-82.

     Accompanied by American business leaders and Detroit's
     carmakers, George Bush's trip to Tokyo had one unique
     mission: to ask for more strenuous trade measures to
     solve the alarming $40 billion trade deficit with Japan.
     Car and car parts account for nearly two-thirds of that
     trade imbalance.   Japanese automakers are eager to
     compromise to prevent tougher American protectionism.

They plan to purchase a significant amount of American-made car parts and components and have agreed to reduce their U.S. auto imports based on the voluntary restraint agreement.

397. Genther, Phyllis A. _A history of Japan's government-business relationship: the passenger car industry_. Ann Arbor, MI: Center for Japanese Studies, The University of Michigan, 1990.

Japanese government-business relationships have been at the center of industrial policy debate for years. At the beginning of the 1980s, the U.S.-Japan automobile crisis heightened the issue of bilateral trade relations. Subsequently researchers drew attention to the potential of the Japanese government-business relationship and its trade policies for increasing the competitiveness of the U.S. auto industry in the global market and for solving social problems related to the automobile. This book investigates the interdependence between the Japanese government and the Japanese automobile industry from the rudimentary stage of the industry to the implementation of the U.S. voluntary export restrictions imposed on the Japanese automobiles in 1981.

398. Greenhouse, Steven. "Trade curbs: do they do the job?" _New York Times_. (April 16, 1992): D1, D10.

This article describes the effects of protectionism on American industries. Except for the motorcycle industry, most economists agree that consumers do not benefit from it. Rather, consumers have to pay higher prices for the same products they used to get. Within the past ten years, Japanese auto imports in the United States increased sharply from 20.5% in 1981 to 30.3% in 1991 since the voluntary restraint agreement went into effect a decade ago. The quotas helped the prosperity of the Japanese auto industry by establishing assembly plants in this country or by joining partnerships with the American companies. Although these Japanese plants helped the U.S. auto industry by creating jobs and promoting industrial development, they also resulted in the most competitive battle between these two nations in the history of American automobile industry.

399. Greenhouse, Steven. "U.S. finds Japan unfair in pricing its minivans." _New York Times_. (May 20, 1992): D1, D7.

The U.S. government reported on May 19, 1992 that Mazda minivans were being sold at 12.5% below their fair value and Toyota vans at 6.75% below fair value. The International Trade Commission is investigating whether such "dumping" has hurt American industry. The dumping case could result in further strain in the trade relations of the two countries.

400. "The House of Representatives passed a bill requiring imported cars to be built with U.S. parts and labor

beginning in 1987." New York Times. (November 4, 1983):
1, 34.

The proposed Senate bill which requires manufacturers
selling more than 100,000 cars per year in the U.S. to
use a specific percentage of U.S. parts and labor based
on units sold is mainly aimed at Japan. Cars made in
Canada are exempted from the above rule because of the
mutual agreement which permits the duty-free sale of cars
made in either country.

401. "The Japan issues Bush forged." Tokyo Business Today.
     60.2 (February 1992): 6-11.

This article discusses the global partnership plans
issued by U.S. President George Bush and Japanese Prime
Minister Kiichi Miyazawa. The primary target of this
program examines the automobile and auto parts industries
which touch upon the following areas: 1) Increasing the
purchase of U.S. auto parts by Japanese assembly plants
operating in the U.S., from about $7 billion in fiscal
1990 to about $15 billion in fiscal 1994; 2) Expanding
local content from about 50% in fiscal 1990 to about 70%
in fiscal 1994; and 3) Doubling Japanese imports of parts
made in America from $2 billion in fiscal 1990 to $4
billion in fiscal 1994.

402. "Japan's car imports, the big stick." Economist.
     332.7741 (January 11, 1992): 60-62.

Following George Bush's visit in Japan accompanied by the
executives of Detroit's Big Three, the situation of trade
imbalances between these two countries has been
intensified. This article analyzes the import and export
trade of the U.S. and Japanese auto industries,
government intervention on auto trade, sales projection
of Japanese imports in America, and future purchasing
plans of the Japanese auto companies.

403. "Japan's labor-intensive, export-oriented auto industry."
     Business Japan. 34.5 (May 1989): 37-49.

The Japanese economy remained stable in 1986. Domestic
demand was still high except that exports of automobiles
was moving slowly due to the higher yen. The auto
industry occupies the highest position in the Japanese
economy because it accounts for the largest percentage of
domestic employment rates, production amounts, equipment
investments, and exports. This article points out
several trade problems the Japanese auto industry
encountered during its period of export expansion. The
voluntary restraint agreement which the Japanese have had
imposed on them since 1981 for the restriction of import
quotas set up by the U.S. government, and the severe
trade imbalances in recent years between the U.S. and
Japan are all difficulties that the Japanese need to
consider and reevaluate.

404. "Japan's minicar market: putt putt." Economist. 314.7645 (March 10, 1990): 76.

Under the Japanese Government Act in 1976, any car with an engine size less than 550 cc, a length less than 3.2 meters and a width less than 1.4 meters would be exempted from Japan's strict parking regulations. Most Japanese people buy minicars in order to take advantage of this as well as for other cost-effective reasons. This situation has been changed since the government's tax reform of 1989 which made the full-sized cars less expensive and more attractive. A major shift in market demand from minicars to upscale models marked the year of 1990. Thus, Japan's minicar producers felt the big slump. This article describes the current Japanese auto-consumption as well as market trend in detail, especially the market shift from minicars to full-sized vehicles.

405. "Japan-U.S. pact draws criticism." Japan Times. 32.3 (January 20-26, 1992): 1, 5.

The trade talks between U.S. President George Bush and Japanese Prime Minister Kiichi Miyazawa in Tokyo are covered in this article. Japanese automakers pledged to purchase $19-billion worth of U.S. auto parts in fiscal 1994 and planned to sell around 20,000 imported U.S. cars annually through their dealerships in Japan within a few years. The two-day summit was highly significant for both governments. The economic accords are meant to produce increased trade between both countries, foster the development of the American auto industry, and create more jobs in the United States.

406. "Japanese government will not agree to a request by the U.S. to revise the current voluntary auto exports agreement for 1982." Automotive News. (December 7, 1981), 1, 44.

Japanese officials did not agree with any further restrictions on vehicular shipments below the 1981 level of 1.68 million and would reject any further reduction of exports to the United States. Imports will need to decline an additional 12.1% in 1981 to reach the voluntary restraint levels. The U.S. Commerce Department projected that the total industry's losses would be $1.4 billion by the end of 1981.

407. Kitazume, Takashi and Hisane Masaki. "Bush visit marks fundamental shift in bilateral relations." Japan Times. 33.3 (1992): 1, 5.

President George Bush's visit to Japan is expected to bring closer political ties in the post-cold war era between these two countries. Japan's automakers agreed to support the ailing U.S. economy as long as the Bush administration offered to help Japan and assumed a greater political role in the global scene. Comments and critical views from top automobile executives on both sides were described in this document.

408. Koepp, Stephen and William McWhirter. "I'm not asking for sympathy." <u>Time</u>. 139 (January 27, 1992): 45-46.

This article includes an interview with the former chief of General Motors, Robert Stempel. It discusses the effect of the current economic recession on the sales of GM cars, and the perception of the U.S. trade mission in Japan on American automakers and the American people. U.S. and Japanese car manufacturers are compared on the issues of labor-management, employee-layoffs, plants-closing, cost-efficiencies and auto-safety.

409. Levin, Doron P. "U.S.-Japan auto chiefs hold talks." <u>New York Times</u>. (May 19, 1992): D1, D9.

The chairmen of the Big Three and the chief executives of the top five Japanese automakers held a meeting in Chicago to discuss the bilateral trade problems between the two countries with the aim of stimulating Japanese purchases of American auto parts and distribution of American autos in Japan. The Japanese automakers pledged to buy $19 billion of American auto parts by 1994 and to help by selling an extra 19,700 American cars annually.

410. Levin, Doron P. "Iacocca urges U.S. limits on Japanese car sales." <u>New York Times</u>. (October 16, 1991): D7.

Motivated by the growing Japanese competition and a weak domestic economy, Chrysler chairman Lee Iacocca urges the U.S. government to put new limits on Japanese car sales in this country. In recent years, Japanese imports have dropped as the number of vehicles produced by their transplants increased. With accumulated losses last year that have totaled around $6 billion, it's time for the ailing American auto industry to react with stricter rules and legislation to be enforced on Japanese imports in this country.

411. Maggs, John. "Bill targets Japanese transplant auto sales." <u>Journal of Commerce and Commercial</u>. 389.27564 (September 17, 1991): 1A, 12A.

The present voluntary export restraint agreement between the United States and Japan is 2.3 million vehicles per year. Due to Detroit's big auto sales slump within the recent couple of years, and the growing trade surplus between these two nations, the U.S. government is planning to draft a comprehensive auto bill that would include the new import restraints and other trade-related measures to force Japan to open its market to U.S. auto companies.

412. Maskery, Mary Ann. "Japan renews export quota for another year at 2.3 million." <u>Automotive News</u>. (January 22, 1990): 48.

After Japan announces that they are going to retain voluntary restrictions on auto exports to the United States for the 9th straight year, with the 1990-1991 limits on 2.3 million cars, various responses and reactions came from big Japanese auto companies. While most Japanese manufacturers criticize this announcement, companies that might be able to sell more cars in the United States--Toyota and Honda--accepted this as a second-best solution.

413. Neff, Robert, Paul Magnusson and Douglas Harbrecht. "How much can Bush bring home?" Business Week. 3247 (January 13, 1992): 44-45.

This article describes President Bush's trade mission to Japan in January 1992 about the economic concessions for nearly three fourths of 1991's $43 billion trade deficit with the country on autos and auto parts industries.

414. Okamoto, Yumiko. An empirical analysis of nontariff barriers and manufactured imports of Japan. Thesis (Ph.D.)--University of Hawaii, 1989.

Over the past few decades, non-tariff barriers have been cited as the predominant cause of Japan's low level of manufactured imports. This research examines the trends in Japan's imports, and analyzes the role of Japan's nontariff barriers in manufactured imports of automobile, textile, and clothing industries.

415. Okawara, Yoshihiro. "U.S. market woes strain Japanese makers in fiscal 1987." Business Japan. 33.11 (November 1988): 141-40.

The overall concern about trade imbalances in automobiles between Japan and the United States is reaching a crucial turning-point. There are two major issues associated with the auto industry problems in the United States: Japan's investment in the automobile and auto parts industries in America, and the promotion of imports of auto parts from the United States. The growing awareness of the problem and the possible solutions and negotiations between these two nations are the major focus of the auto industry.

416. "Once more, with backing." Time. 139 (June 1, 1992): 24-26.

The U.S. and Japanese automakers met in May 1992 in Chicago to discuss the $43 billion trade deficit between the two countries, nearly one-thirds of which comes from Japanese auto products. It is expected that a certain degree of recognition on both sides and the need for accommodation between the two countries be achieved.

417. Powell, Bill. "Detroit pleads its case." Newsweek. 117 (April 8, 1991): 42.

In a meeting with President Bush, Chrysler's Chief Lee Iacocca pleaded with him to set up a new limit on Japan's increasing share of the U.S. auto market. The auto executive from Detroit requested the government to

conform with new auto emission standards and argued
against the proposals to raise the average fuel
efficiency required by automakers on all of their
vehicles.

418. Rauch, Jonathan. "Drive shaft: why GM can't compete in
Tokyo." The New Republic. 206 (April 13, 1992): 15-16.

This paper discusses the intricate U.S.-Japanese auto
trade relations. The author points out several factors
which prevent the Big Three from entering the Japanese
auto market. For example, American cars have image and
quality problems, distribution problems, and they are
unfit for the Japanese auto market. The major reason is
the position of steering wheels. Japanese cars follow
right-hand-drive pattern. However, none of the Big Three
has set up concrete plans to make the U.S.-made
right-hand-drive cars available in Japan.

419. A Review of recent developments in the U.S. automobile
industry including an assessment of the Japanese
voluntary restraint agreements: preliminary report to the
Subcommittee on Trade, Committee on Ways and Means, of
the U.S. House of Representatives in connection with
investigation no. 332-188. Washington, DC: U.S.
International Trade Commission, [1985].

This paper includes information to assist in future
decisions regarding any extension of the automobile
voluntary restraint agreement (VRA) with Japan. Many
developments influenced the U.S. automobile industry
during 1981-1984, including changes in consumer demand,
fluctuations in gasoline prices, and the increasing
number of joint venture arrangements between the U.S. and
foreign auto companies. Of the factors influencing the
industry during this period, the principal was the
initiation of the VRA with Japan. This paper reviews
developments in the U.S. automobile industry in recent
years and attempts to quantify the effects of the VRA on
the U.S. automobile industry, employment, and consumers
during 1981-84.

420. Ries, John Charles. Vertical differentiation, quotas,
and profits: voluntary export restraints on Japanese
automobiles. Thesis (Ph.D.)--The University of Michigan,
1990.

This dissertation includes three parts which discuss the
effect of voluntary export restraints on the
profitability of firms in the Japanese auto industry.

421. Sanger, David E. "Is 'local content' the smartest way to
judge imports?" New York Times. (March 8, 1992): E3.

"Local content" rules remain a source of debate between
the U.S. and Japanese auto industries. The issue was
stirred up on the surface when the Bush Administration
ruled that the Honda Civics assembled in Canada do not

meet the 50% or more "North American content" requirement
and hence they do not qualify for duty-free treatment.

422. Sanger, David E.   "Japan's gift to Bush: trying to
     forestall trade restrictions, Tokyo to cut ceiling on
     auto exports." New York Times. (March 20, 1992): D1,
     D9.

     Japan has imposed the tightest limits in the 12-year
     history of the voluntary export restraints effected since
     1981. The Ministry of International Trade and Industry
     announced that the new limit on auto exports to the
     United States would be set at 1.65 million beginning on
     April 1, 1992. Detroit's automakers did not seem to be
     pleased by this decision. They claimed that the limit
     only applied to cars actually shipped from Japan.
     However, its transplant production in the U.S far
     outstripped the volume of its new export restraint
     quotas.

423. Skrentny, Roger.   "Japan takes Detroit for a ride."
     Marketing Communications. 12.4 (April 1987): 70-76, 86.

     The voluntary restraint agreement (VRA) which went into
     effect in 1981 was initially planned to limit Japanese
     import quotas in order to let U.S. automakers catch up
     with the Japanese in the small car market. However, the
     VRA really gave the Japanese a great chance to stabilize
     their production and reach the upscale car market.
     Forced to limit their export volume, the Japanese auto
     manufacturers began to replace their small, compact cars
     with larger, more expensive ones.   Under the
     circumstances, Japan's big four automakers--Toyota,
     Nissan, Honda, and Mazda are all on their way to changing
     their global export strategies in order to produce
     sporty, luxurious models to gain more sales in the U.S.
     auto market.

424. Sterngold, James.   "The quandary in Japan."   New York
     Times. (January 16, 1992): A1, A12.

     This article reports President Bush's visit to Japan with
     the top executives of the Big Three concerning trade
     negotiations between these two countries on auto-related
     issues.   There were two agreements being reached.   The
     first one was the "Tokyo Declaration". It outlined the
     relations between the two countries in the postwar era on
     political, security, and economic issues. The second one
     was an "Action Plan" concerning Japan's specific
     responses to American complaints about trade and a
     campaign to buy more U.S. autos and auto parts.

425. Symonds, William C.   "Gunfight at the Customs corral."
     Business Week. 3254 (March 2, 1992): 54.

     In February 12, 1992, the U.S. Customs Service levied
     taxes on Honda Civics imported in 1989-90 for $19 million
     in back duties. Customs said that Civics built that year
     failed to meet the 50% North American content requirement

of the US-Canada Free Trade Agreement. That ruling is
likely to have a far-reaching impact on free trade in
North America.

426. Taylor, Alex III. "Do you know where your car was made?"
     Fortune. 123 (June 17, 1991): 52-56.

     The U.S. law that regulates the corporate average fuel
     economy (CAFE) standards has been criticized for a long
     time by the entire auto-industrial field.   The law
     encourages automakers to play games with the domestic
     content legislation (a car with 75% or more U.S. or
     Canadian content is considered domestic) in order to
     avoid fines set up by the CAFE standards. This situation
     eventually results in Japanese automakers' buying less
     U.S.-made auto parts. The domestic content legislation
     is also a debatable issue. The law does not really look
     at where the pieces are made as far as they have been
     "substantially transformed" in the United States.   The
     provision irritates U.S. auto parts makers and consumers
     alike.

427. Taylor, Alex III.   "Ford to the feds: help Detroit."
     Fortune. 124.6 (September 9, 1991): 131-34.

     Harold Poling, CEO of Ford Motor Co., thinks that the
     automobile industry is in the most challenging period it
     has ever confronted. In an interview, Poling argues that
     while Detroit has to take some of the blame for its own
     slowdown, government policies have contributed.   His
     appeal to President Bush includes: a slowdown in
     regulations, trade action against Japan, and increased
     economic stimulus.

428. Treece, James B. and Karen Lowry Miller.   "If the
     Japanese were running GM." Business Week. 3249 (January
     27, 1992): 32.

     Compares government practices and assistance offered to
     a troubled auto company in the United States with the
     parallel situation and reactions in Japan. In the United
     States, General Motors, with its slumping 1991 auto sales
     and an estimated $6 billion loss in the North American
     market, will have to close six assembly plants and
     fifteen parts plants in the United States within the next
     four years. In Japan, a troubled company is expected to
     fix its own problems with assistance from supporting
     companies in its keiretsu (group affiliation centered
     around a bank where most major companies are a member).
     In GM's circumstances, banks will take actions early on
     instead of waiting for troubles to show up.   The
     close-knit government and business relationship in Japan
     and the Japanese keiretsu play key roles in the Japanese
     automobile industry today.   The same practice may not
     work for the American auto industry because of the
     differences in cultural and social background as well as
     in government policies.

429. United States. Congress. Senate. Committee on Commerce.
     Subcommittee on Surface Transportation. <u>Automobile fuel
     economy and research and development: hearings before the
     Committee   on   Commerce,   United   States   Senate,
     Ninety-fourth Congress, first session...March 12 and 13,
     1975</u>. Washington, DC: U.S. Government Printing Office,
     1975.

     The substantial increase in gasoline prices that followed
     the 1973 oil embargo changed auto buyers' attitude toward
     purchasing small, fuel-efficient Japanese-made cars. At
     that time, President Carter's automotive energy proposals
     and the Energy Policy and Conservation Act were all
     concentrated on the issue of a future automotive fuel
     economy. This report discusses the major impact of the
     government's   price   incentives   to   reduce   gasoline
     consumption, and the consequences of a big shift in
     American auto-purchasing patterns from U.S. cars to
     Japanese cars.

430. United States. Congress. Senate. Committee on Banking,
     Housing, and Urban Affairs. Subcommittee on Economic
     Stabilization. <u>The effect of expanding Japanese
     automobile imports on the domestic economy: hearing
     before the Subcommittee on Economic Stabilization of the
     Committee on Banking, Housing, and Urban Affairs, United
     States Senate, Ninety-sixth Congress, second session,
     April 3, 1980</u>. Washington, DC: U.S. Government Printing
     Office, 1980.

     Facing the sharply rising sales of Japanese automobile
     imports, the American automotive industry is today in the
     midst of a dramatic transition. This transition is
     particularly difficult for workers in the industry.
     Several problems and probable solutions are discussed in
     this Congressional hearing. Emphasis is placed on the
     auto-trade,   employment,   foreign   investment,   and
     international trade barriers.

431. United States. Congress. House. Committee on Energy and
     Commerce. Subcommittee on Commerce, Transportation, and
     Tourism. <u>Future of the automobile industry: hearing
     before the Subcommittee on Commerce, Transportation, and
     Tourism of the Committee on Energy and Commerce, House of
     Representatives, Ninety-eighth Congress, second session,
     February 8, 1984</u>. Washington, DC: U.S. Government
     Printing Office, 1984.

     This document addresses the future of the automobile
     industry in light of the FTC (Federal Trade Commission).
     The objectives of this report are two-fold: one is to get
     the facts so we can understand the implications of the
     potentially far-reaching trends that are emerging today
     in the auto industry; the second one is to ask what is
     the best way of dealing with these trends. This report
     reviews these industry developments with an eye toward
     their long-range impact, not only on the economy, but
     also on American jobs and American consumers.

432. United States. Congress. House. Committee on Ways and
     Means. Japanese voluntary restraints on auto exports to
     the United States: hearings before the Subcommittee on
     Trade of the Committee on Ways and Means, House of
     Representatives, Ninety-ninth Congress, first session,
     February 28 and March 4, 1985. Washington, DC: U.S.
     Government Printing Office, 1985.

     This document explores automotive protectionism which is
     a major American public policy issue. The imported
     automobile industry in America currently operates under
     these two measures: decrease the availability of imported
     vehicles and increase the cost of imported automobiles.
     While the discussion underway will focus on encouraging
     consumers to purchase domestic vehicles, major changes in
     the tax rates on motor vehicles, labor markets, employee
     income taxes, have to be implemented.

433. United States. Congress. Joint Economic Committee.
     Subcommittee on Trade, Productivity, and Economic Growth.
     The legacy of the Japanese voluntary export restraints:
     hearing before the Subcommittee on Trade, Productivity,
     and Economic Growth of the Joint Economic Committee,
     Congress of the United States, Ninety-ninth Congress,
     first session, June 24, 1985. Washington, DC: U.S.
     Government Printing Office, 1986.

     In 1981, the United States entered into a voluntary
     export restraint arrangement with Japan for the purpose
     of temporarily reducing that nation's automotive exports
     to the United States. The hearing, which includes
     questions and discussions, is focused on how to implement
     an appropriate U.S. trade policy and a re-evaluation of
     current industrial policies in order to relieve the
     competition between U.S. auto industry with Japanese auto
     exports.

434. United States. Congress. Senate. Select Committee on
     Small Business. Small business automobile dealers their
     status and the impact of foreign auto imports on them :
     hearings before the Select Committee on Small Business,
     United States Senate, Ninety-sixth Congress, second
     session...April 3 and 21, 1980. Washington, DC: U.S.
     Government Printing Office, 1980.

     The oil crisis of the early 1980s created a major shift
     for consumers toward the purchase of smaller, more fuel
     efficient Japanese cars. Thus, the large inventory of
     American cars created a big financial burden for small
     automobile dealers. A steady growth in dealerships
     offering Japanese cars outweighed the overall number of
     American-car dealers. Chrysler dealers faced severe
     financial difficulties at this time. This study was
     mandated by the Chrysler Corporation Loan Guaranty Act
     under Section 17 which required that a study be conducted
     by the Small Business Administration on the financial
     problems faced by small auto dealers. In this report,
     the status and impact of Japanese imported cars on the
     American automarket, especially on U.S. small business

auto dealers is fully analyzed, and the economic assistance provided by the government is also described.

435. United States. Congress. Joint Economic Committee. U.S. trade and investment policy: imports and the future of the American automobile industry: hearing before the Joint Economic Committee, Congress of the United States, Ninety-sixth Congress, second session, March 19, 1980. Washington, DC: U.S. Government Printing Office, 1980.

In the 1980's, the American auto market suffered from the most severe decline of auto sales in its history, and consequently more than 200,000 American auto workers were faced with layoffs and job losses. The big issue in U.S. trade and investment policy, and the lucrative Japanese auto industry became the central theme of this document. Control of Japanese imports is necessary. In order to save the American auto market, government policy has to be set up, and strict rules and regulations must be imposed on Japanese import sales. The purpose of this hearing is to find the remedial measures to solve this problem.

436. "United States will seek continued curbs on Japan's cars: but Reagan wants to hold exports at higher level than in previous years." Wall Street Journal. (October 19, 1983): 41.

The tightened rule imposed by the Reagan Administration would hold the voluntary export restraints for Japanese autos to 1.8 million per year, up from the 1.68 million per year since 1981. United States automakers had different reactions to this. General Motors wanted to raise Japanese exports to get as many Japanese-made units from its Japanese affiliates as possible. Others would prefer to remain at the lowest levels.

437. Washio, Ako and Emiko Ohi. "Cut in auto export quota may backfire." Japan Times. 32.13 (March 30, 1992): 1, 6.

Japan's Ministry of International Trade and Industry recently announced that the quota would be adjusted from 2.3 million to 1.65 million vehicles from April 1, 1992. Initially set at 1.68 million vehicles in 1981, the voluntary quota was raised in 1984 and 1985 as Japan's U.S. auto production increased. The Big Three U.S. automakers did not seem to be pleased with the 650,000 unit cut, they have submitted a bill to the U.S. Congress to call for restraints on both locally produced and imported Japanese cars.

438. Washio, Ako and Emiko Ohki. "Real results of action plan for automobile trade unclear." Japan Times. 32.3 (January 20-26, 1992): 17.

Covers a discussion on the recent U.S.-Japanese action plan to increase Japanese imports of U.S. auto parts and finished automobiles. The goals of the plan include increasing automobile imports to 19,700 units by fiscal

1995 and doubling the value of auto parts imports to
$19.1 billion in fiscal 1994. The Japanese auto industry
leaders are not quite confident about meeting these
targets. They have required that U.S. automakers push to
produce more attractive models for the choosy Japanese
consumers.

439. Winham, Gilbert R.   The automobile trade crisis of 1980.
Halifax, Canada: Centre for Foreign Policy Studies, 1981.

In 1980, the American automobile industry entered an era
of trade crisis with Japan. The major reasons for the
difficulties of the domestic auto industry are the
effects of recession, the rapid rise of gasoline prices,
and the uncertainty about future gasoline supplies. The
effects of these factors shifted consumer demand sharply
from large to small fuel-efficient cars.   Specific
economic problems escalated the political confrontations
between the two countries. On May 1, 1981, the Japanese
government reached an agreement with the U.S. to restrict
voluntarily their auto exports to the United States to
1.68 million vehicles in 1981, down from the 1.82 million
shipped in 1980. The impact of this voluntary restraint
agreement on the U.S. auto industry and U.S.-Japan
economic relations, as well as on American government
policy are all discussed in this book.

440. Winston, Clifford.   Blind intersection? Policy and the
automobile industry.   Washington, DC: The Brookings
Institution, 1987.

This book first examines the cost competitiveness of the
U.S. auto industry and its market demand forecasts, then
it puts major emphasis on the analysis of U.S. government
regulations for automobile safety, fuel efficiency, speed
limit, and the voluntary export restrictions.   The
primary purpose of the book is to evaluate these
government policies for increasing the competitiveness of
U.S. automobile manufacturers on the foreign market and
for solving social problems related to the automobile.
Comparative analyses of U.S. and Japanese auto industries
are fully covered in this book as well.

7

Case Studies

441. Anzai, Tatsuya. "A cool reception for MMC." Tokyo Business Today. (January 1989): 58-59.

    Describes and projects the business situation of Mitsubishi Motors Corp. (MMC). During the fiscal year 1988, the company called for sales of 1.86 trillion yen, and current profits of 33 billion yen, both were record-highs. However, the chances of maintaining the pace is rare. Due to the market fluctuations and growing international competition, MMC's export ratio is projected to drop below 50% in fiscal year 1989, and the possibility of export growth from now on is slight. The goal of the company is to strengthen its creative and independent management strategy based upon its recent Japanese stock market listing.

442. Armstrong, Larry. "The American drivers steering Japan through the states." Business Week. 3149 (March 12, 1990): 98-99.

    Robert B. McCurry, Thomas G. Elliott, and Thomas D. Mignanelli, as the three top American executives at Toyota, Honda, and Nissan, respectively, tell us the success stories of these Japanese companies, and their public images and personal influences on these companies.

443. Armstrong, Larry, Leslie Helm and James Treece B., et al. "Toyota's fast lane: frugal, reclusive commanders of an industrial army." Business Week. 2919 (November 4, 1985): 42-46.

    Toyota Motor Corporation is planning to replace General Motors Corporation as the world's leading auto manufacturer. It controls 42% of the Japanese market and

presently sells more cars in the U.S. than any other
foreign automaker. The company has formed a joint
venture with GM to establish a "just-in-time" production
system and to bring its parts suppliers to the U.S.
Toyota City, Japan, is the headquarters of the company.
The Toyota empire controls over 3% of Japan's gross
national product. Currently, the company's chairman is
President Shoichiro Toyoda, who is the son of Toyota's
founder, Mr. Eiji Toyoda.

444. Barrett, Amy.   "Beating the odds."   Financial World.
     159.25 (December 11, 1990): 30-32.

A case study of Arvin Industries, the U.S. auto parts
supplier, is included in this article. The impact of
Japanese suppliers in the United states and the
increasingly stringent standards faced by Japanese and
U.S. customers are the major concerns of the company.
Improvement has been made. However, the ongoing
competition will make the company even tougher to fight
for better quality products for its customers in order to
win good business in the auto supplies industry.

445. Borrus, Amy, Mark Maremont and William J. Hampton.
     "Japanese car wars have Nissan biting the bullet."
     Business Week. 2976 (December 8, 1986): 52-53.

The number two Japanese automaker, Nissan Motor Co.,
reported an operating loss of $121.9 million for the
first time since 1951 during the six months ended
September 30, 1986. The main financial loss in the U.S.
is due to the poor sales of trucks and sports cars. At
the same time, the big battle with Toyota in Japan is
also getting tense. The company's best hope now seems to
be the European market.

446. Caplen, Brian.   "Staying ahead by following."   Asian
     Business. 26.4 (April 1990): 24-30.

Toyota Motor Corp., Japan's largest auto producer, has
earned the reputation of letting other companies take
risks with new models and overseas ventures before
following in their ways. With an 8.1% share of the world
vehicle market, Toyota ranks the third in world output
behind General Motors (16.6%) and Ford (13.3%). The
detailed description of Toyota's production management,
manufacturing system, overseas expansion plan, product
development, and upscale market are examined.

447. Chandler, Clay.   "It's hello dollies at Nissan's new
     'dream factory'." Wall Street Journal. (July 6, 1992):
     A13, A20.

Nissan Motor Co.'s new "flexible-manufacturing system"
that allows one single assembly facility to build a wide
variation of models and types of cars at high speed on
one assembly line at its "dream factory" in Kyushu,
Japan, is discussed. When fully implemented, the Kyushu
plant will be able to build four models in eight

different body types at a rate of near 240,000 vehicles annually. The primary goal of the system is to improve Nissan's ability to respond quickly and efficiently to consumer demands.

448. Flint, Jerry. "The new number three?" Forbes. 145.12 (June 11, 1990): 136-40.

Toyota's cars are so popular these days that they may take the number three position in the U.S. market, ahead of Honda and Chrysler. In addition to a hard working crew and the high quality of its products, the company's success in the U.S. market should in part be attributed to its vice president, Robert McCurry. Under his personal influence, Toyota has been moving towards a younger, sportier look. McCurry's goal is to sell 1.5 million cars and trucks in 1995. The company may need to invest and build more plants in the U.S. in order to reach that projected figure.

449. Fucini, Joseph J. and Suzy Fucini. Working for the Japanese: inside Mazda's American auto plant. New York, NY: The Free Press, 1990.

The authors conducted more than 150 interviews with managers and workers at the Mazda-Flat Rock plant, union officials, state and local government executives, and citizens of the Downriver area. This book is the end product of this research. It focuses on the discussion of the distinctive Japanese culture which is carried out in the Mazda plant. The spirit of the Japanese workforce is expressed through labor management, a "just-in-time" system, job loyalty, lifetime employment, and coordination between workers and managers. This case study describes in detail the daily activities in the Mazda plant in Flat Rock, Michigan.

450. Fujiwara, Yasunobu. "Isuzu on a bumpy road paved with problems." Tokyo Business Today. 60.1 (January 1992): 32-33.

Isuzu Motors Ltd. is facing problems in its corporate affairs. Poor domestic car sales in Japan, unprofitable operations in the United States, and the deficit operation of Subaru-Isuzu Automotive Inc's plant in America are all factors contributing to the company's poor performance record in 1991. Although General Motors is the leading shareholder in Isuzu, with 37% of its stock, the company has not drafted any clear assistance measures for Isuzu yet. Under the present circumstances, Isuzu has decided to use its limited resources to sustain its current business and at the same time reconstruct its passenger car sector which is one of the weakest areas for the company's domestic car sales.

451. Gabel, H. Landis and Anthony E. Hall. "The Nissan Corporation." Journal of Management Case Studies. 1.2 (Summer 1985): 97-101.

The early development of the Japanese automobile industry
and the case study of Nissan Motor Co. are covered.

452. "Hello, dollies!: factory automation."   Industry Week.
     (September 7, 1992): 39, 46.

     Nissan Motor Co. Ltd.'s new automobile facility in Kyushu
     is one of the best Japanese plants that have been built
     with their workers in mind. With an annual capacity of
     600,000 vehicles, the plant is equipped with the
     Intelligent Body Assembly System (IBAS) that performs the
     initial welds in body assembly. The system can be
     retooled by changing the software, which significantly
     reduces retooling time and increases welding accuracy.
     The plant exhibits a concern for the global environment
     by using natural gas to gain efficiency and cleaner
     emissions. The Kyushu plant also pays great attention to
     a worker-friendly environment which is reflected in its
     plant layout and workplace atmosphere. In view of the
     labor-shortage problem which prevails in the Japanese
     automobile industry, Nissan is planning to implement
     extensive automation to attract older members of Japan's
     workforce and to employ the handicapped.

453. Higurashi, Ryoichi. "Honda Motor loses no. 3 spot and
     its founder." Tokyo Business Today.   59.10 (October
     1991): 23.

     A biographical sketch of Mr. Soichiro Honda, founder of
     Honda Motor Co. who died at age of 84, and the business
     conditions of the company are offered in this article.
     Honda held the number three position for Japan's
     automotive sales in 1989. Due to the big slump in its
     domestic sales and the weakness of its sales network, the
     company was outstripped by Mitsubishi Motors Corp. and
     Mazda Motor Corp., falling into 5th place in 1990. Honda
     is planning to develop highly distinctive and upscale
     models as its recent catch-up strategy on the domestic
     market.

454. Hill, Richard Child, Michael Indergrad and Kuniko Fujita.
     "Flat Rock, home of Mazda: the social impact of a
     Japanese company on an American community." In The auto
     industry ahead: who's driving?. Arnesen, Peter J., ed.
     Ann Arbor, MI: Center for Japanese Studies, The
     University of Michigan, 1989, pp. 69-131.

     This case study describes the social impact of the Mazda
     Motor Corp. in Flat Rock, Michigan, on the local
     Downriver community through personal interviews carried
     out by the authors. Five major areas are analyzed in
     this study: 1) The parent auto company: emphasis is
     placed on the interpersonal relations between Mazda Motor
     Corp. and its employees; 2) The union: Mazda's experience
     of joining the UAW forms a new wave of labor-management
     relations among the Japanese firms; 3) Suppliers: debates
     concentrate on the quality issue of U.S. versus Japanese
     products and the Japanese relationship with U.S.
     suppliers; 4) Government: Mazda's investment in Flat

Rock, Michigan, brought up complex intergovernmental issues; the role of the transplant and its regional impact on the local community are discussed; and 5) Community: the economic impact on the changes of the local real-estate values and housing development as well as the Japanese cultural influences are analyzed.

455. "Honda to expand site at $240 million cost: plans US-built Civic." Wall Street Journal. (January 11, 1984): 2.

Honda Motor Co. will invest $240 million to expand its Marysville, Ohio, plant. The expansion plan will start in early 1984, with a projected goal of producing 300,000 cars per year, doubling its present capacity. The company plans to begin U.S. production of its Civic model by mid-1986.

456. "Honda's way: Japanese car makers in America." Economist. (November 28, 1992): 76-77.

This article describes the operation, design and quality control issues of Honda's American transplant built in Marysville, Ohio. As the leading Japanese automaker who pioneered the "transplant" factory in America, Honda has successfully set up its automobile operations in the United States. The company has invested more than $3 billion in its American productions with the current employment figure close to 15,000 people. Honda's Accord has been the best-selling car for the past two years. Now it faces a challenge from 1992 Ford's Taurus. New designs of the Accord station wagon and minivan would be the company's next step in seeking long-term improvement and customer satisfaction.

457. Horton, Cleveland. "Mitsubishi maps solo success." Advertising Age. 61.27 (July 2, 1990): 3, 33.

Mitsubishi Motors Corp., the number four importer of Japanese automobiles, has slowly been building up its auto empire in America since its establishment of independent marketing firms in the United States in 1981. In recent years, Mitsubishi has been putting a strong dealer organization in the South and Midwest, and has been investing heavily in advertising to attract car buyers. The company plans to introduce four new models in 1991: the 3000 GT sports car, a restyled Sigma luxury sedan, a redesigned Montero sports-utility vehicle, and two new versions of its van.

458. Inaba, Yu. "Nissan's management revolution." Tokyo Business Today. 57.10 (October 1989): 38-40.

Nissan Motor Co. Ltd. has experienced dramatic improvement since the appointment of a new president, Yutaka Kume, in June 1985. He hired an outside consultant from McKinsey & Co. to completely reorganize the company and to apply a concept called "product market strategy," which stresses reforming the entire corporate

culture. Comments and inputs from Nissan's younger staff
have also made a considerable contribution to the
company's continuous progress. Kume's management
strategies, combined with the initiatives of top and
middle management, have halted Nissan's declining market
share.

459. Ishizuna, Yasuhiro. "The transformation of Nissan: the
     reform of corporate culture." Long Range Planning. 23.3
     (June 1990): 9-15.

     Nissan Motor Co. experienced severe ups and downs in the
     1980s. The company was affected by dropping sales and
     labor-management conflicts. In 1985, Nissan's new
     president, Mr. Yutaka Kume, started directing his
     energies toward a reform of the company's systems and
     corporate culture. The gradual improvement achieved
     tangible results. With the development of the Be-1
     model, followed by Japan's first personal luxury sedan
     called Cima, the domestic market regained its strong
     position. Nissan's persistent effort to promote
     "localization" in its overseas operations, and the
     globalization of the company's operations led to the
     inauguration of a new organization which transformed
     every area of the company.

460. "Japan's car makers: Honda loses its way." Economist.
     320.7724 (September 14, 1991): 79-80.

     Honda Motor Co., Japan's third-largest automaker, has
     been on the decline. Without best-selling pickup trucks
     or new upscale models to counter those of Toyota, Honda
     lost 0.5% of market share in Japan, to 7.3% in 1990. For
     auto sales in America, where Honda Accord was the best-
     selling car in 1990, Honda is about to be overtaken by
     Toyota. In order to counter this trend, Honda plans to
     introduce a top-down management style to replace the
     traditional consensus approach of decision-making
     processes. The company also wants to develop new car
     models and to upgrade its aging factories built in
     America.

461. "The Japanese approach: the shape of things to come."
     Production. 97.5 (May 1986): 69-70.

     Mazda Motor Corp.'s Hofu plant in Japan uses advanced
     materials-handling systems, robotics, and other
     production improvement methods in body assembly and
     materials handling. The plant has upgraded its systems
     functions using advanced technologies to promote its
     flexibility, efficiency, and quality. It has also created
     a clean and pleasant work environment for factory
     workers.

462. Johnstone, Bob. "A question of balance: Honda jostles
     for pole position in race to build car of tomorrow." Far
     Eastern Economic Review. 155.20 (May 21, 1992): 40-45.

Honda Motor Co. Ltd., the third largest Japanese automaker, has performed quite well in a weak global auto market. The real challenge for the company in 1990s is how it responds to the environmental and technological concerns in the company's future product development and production technology. There are three major areas in particular which need to be balanced: 1) Markets: Honda cars should meet the different needs of U.S. and Japanese clients; 2) Materials: the company must balance the choices of steel with plastics and aluminum; and 3) Engines: Honda must balance fuel-economy and environmental concerns with driving performance.

463. Kaneko, Shozo. "Honda steps on the gas: experiment to prevent 'big business disease'." Business Japan. 32.2 (February 1987): 23-28.

Honda Motor Co., a latecomer to the passenger car market, achieved a good reputation in distinctive design, product quality, and creative style. The company encourages its employees to exchange personal views with great freedom. It is also experimenting with participatory management by supervisory level workers. New ideas and strategies emerge constantly since the executives exchange views with the workers.

464. King, John. "Mazda, American style." CFO: The Magazine for Chief Financial Officers. 6.7 (July 1990): 28-33.

Tim Sullivan, the controller of Mazda Inc. in Irvine, California, describes his personal view as a corporate leader coping with both Japanese and American industrial cultures. In general, the Japanese focus on long-range planning rather than quarterly results and stress group consensus instead of independent decision-making. The Japanese companies and their employees form a strong bond and a partnership while the Americans do not.

465. Kotkin, Joel. "Mr. Iacocca meets Mr. Honda." Inc. 8.11 (November 1986): 37-40.

A comparative analysis of Honda Motor Co. Ltd., built by Soichiro Honda, and Chrysler Motors Corp., led by Lee Iacocca, is presented in terms of company operations, automobile businesses, and joint ventures.

466. Kurihara, Shohei. "Toyota in the era of internationalization." Management Japan. 23.2 (Autumn 1990): 3-9.

Toyota Motor Corp. plans to implement the following steps for future development: 1) creating demand, 2) cooperating with other manufacturers, 3) contributing to host countries and regions, 4) paying greater attention to each country's economy, and 5) addressing global environmental concerns. The company plans to strengthen economic ties with the Asian-Pacific nations and to

accommodate its managerial style to the international
environment.

467. Levin, Doron P.   "Toyota plant in Kentucky is font of
     ideas for U.S." New York Times. (May 5, 1992): A1, D8.

     A case study of Toyota Motor Corp. in Georgetown,
     Kentucky, is presented. The major assets of Toyota's
     production   techniques   include: "just-in-time"
     inventories, zero defects and continuous improvement.
     Toyota's lean production process and Henry Ford's mass
     production principles are compared and fully analyzed.
     Also included is the 75% local content dispute involving
     Toyota's Camry line and the description of Toyota's
     non-union approach toward its workers.

468. Levin, Doron P.   "Mitsubishi's big campaign in
     U.S." New York Times. (April 30, 1991): D1, D4.

     In a challenge to U.S. automakers, Mitsubishi Motors
     Corp. keeps expanding its stronghold position in the
     United States. The variety of cars and models introduced
     by the company has almost doubled to nine in less than
     two years. Mitsubishi's new entry in the upscale market
     is a $28,000 Diamonte luxury sedan. The company's joint
     venture with Chrysler is likely to be changed.
     Mitsubishi is negotiating with Chrysler to buy Chrysler's
     50% stake in the assembly plant in Bloomington, Illinois.

469. Levin, Doron P.   "Nissan prospers despite errors." New
     York Times. (May 9, 1990): D1, D3.

     Nissan Motor Co. has gone through several unsuccessful
     attempts in the auto business. The company introduced a
     minivan with very low sales volume, failed to accommodate
     to changes in American taste and underwent a name change
     from Datsun to Nissan that isolated some dealers and
     confused customers. Despite all the difficulties, Nissan
     has demonstrated an ability to correct these mistakes
     quickly and to recover from such incidents. The company
     plans to reduce its design cycle from the current three
     or four years to two years so that new models would fit
     the consumers' tastes better. Nissan also wants to
     increase its share of the U.S. car market to 8% from the
     current 4.7%. To accomplish this, the company has
     doubled its production capacity at the assembly plant in
     Smyrna, Tennessee.

470. Macaulary, C. Diane.   The product cycle and the
     international political economy: a case study of the
     automobile industry. Thesis (Ph.D.)--Claremont Graduate
     School, 1987.

     The product cycle theory, as developed by Raymond Vernon
     in 1966, has been applied by various industries. This
     research examines the automobile industry in Japan, the
     United States, and other European countries for evidence
     of the entire product cycle sequence from innovation,
     production, export volume, and trade to investment.

471. Marumo, Nagayuki. "Nissan's philosophy of vehicle development." Business Japan. 34.11 (November 1989): 48-49.

Nissan Motor Co. Ltd. has gone through miraculous progress in recent years. There are three main ideas that form the basis of Nissan's philosophy of vehicle development: 1) creating cars based on fine-tuned marketing; 2) developing cars backed by superior technology; and 3) engineering cars with people in mind. Nissan announced its new UV-X model, a high performance passenger car which combines beauty and comfort and offers customers a new dimension in driving pleasure.

472. Maskery, Mary Ann. "Honda picks leaders with U.S. savvy." Automotive News. (May 14, 1990): 1+.

Following Tadashi Kume's retirement, the newly selected president of Honda Motor Co. is Nobuhiko Kawamoto, 54, the former head of Honda R & D Co. This article presents a personal profile of the new president and discusses the goals and managerial policies of the company.

473. "Mazda on comback trail." Tokyo Business Today. (September 1989): 48-50.

Mazda Motor Corp., which was affected by the first oil crisis in 1973, and subsequently by the high rise of the yen in 1985, is now on the road to recovery. Due to strong domestic market demand and expanded auto sales with the operation of Mazda Motor Manufacturing USA Co. (MMUC), established in 1987, the company achieved a favorable performance record in fiscal 1988. Mazda has added two more sales channels, Eunos and Autozama, to enhance its market sales network. Eunos will specialize in promoting upscale European-style cars, while Autozama will focus on compact and lightweight vehicles.

474. Meyer, Richard. "Assembly: Mazda." Financial World. 161.8 (April 14, 1992): 46.

Mazda Motor Corp. has changed its goal from achieving zero defects, super efficiency and quick model changeovers into providing factory workers with a more pleasant work environment through automating the final assembly. At Mazda's new Hofu plant, there are plans to automate over half of the final assembly processes by the year 2000. Japan's overemphasis on body assembly and ignorance of human effort elsewhere were the major factors that affected the company's market growth in the early years. Mazda plans to catch up with the current market trend through automating the final assembly line processes as its primary focus.

475. Meyer, Richard. "Systems integration: Toyota." Financial World. 161.8 (April 14, 1992): 44.

From inception to production, it takes 43 months for Toyota Motors to bring a model into the showroom, while in the United States and Europe, automakers need over 60 months. This article describes the automobile design and engineering process, cost distribution and producer-supplier relationships at Toyota. It also details the company's complete automobile development processes and its unique kanban system.

476. Meyer, Richard. "Of cars and curry." _Financial World_. 158.15 (July 25, 1989): 38-39.

The improvement of Nissan Motor Co. during recent years has been spectacular. Although the company had suffered from big operating losses in 1989, its instant recovery from the appreciating yen was the greatest feat that enabled the company to replace Toyota and Honda as the industry leader. The goal of the company is to put major emphasis on design for the tastes of local consumers, and to strengthen its sales and marketing force in the domestic market in order to meet the challenge of 1991.

477. Miller, Karen Lowry. "Honda's nightmare: maybe you can't go home again." _Business Week_. 3193 (December 24, 1990): 36.

Honda leads in U.S. auto sales, and its Accord model is the best-selling car in America. However, its success in the U.S. cannot gain the same appeal in its own fashion-conscious country. The Japanese economy is winding down, deflating the auto boom of the past few years. Honda plans to add an additional 10,000 workers into its sales and customer services. It is not an easy task in the current tight labor market and economic downturn.

478. Miller, Karen Lowry and Larry Armstrong. "Will Nissan get it right this time?" _Business Week_. (April 20, 1992): 82-87.

Nissan Motor Co. has passed through a series of major changes in order to guide the company away from a decade of failures. From 1980 to 1991, Nissan's U.S. market share dropped from 5.5% to 4.7%, while Japan's overall share of the U.S. market grew from 17.7% to 28.5%. There are several major issues which the company needs to focus on: 1) Pay more attention to customer's needs, 2) Provide the right product at the right time, and 3) Meet the changing needs of local market requirements and new model design. Nissan is planning to reorganize its U.S. auto sales and produce family sedans and minivans to deal with the current economic downturn. The company is launching Altima, a new sedan a price of around $14,000, to compete with Honda's Accord and Toyota's Camry.

479. Niland, Powell. "Case study: U.S.-Japanese joint venture: New United Motor." _Planning Review_. 17.1 (January/February 1989): 40-45.

The New United Motor Manufacturing Inc. (NUMMI) was created in February 1983 by the joint collaboration of

General Motors Corp. and Toyota Motor Corp. in Fremont, California. The joint venture provides the chance for both Toyota and GM to learn each other's corporate management, union versus non-union approach, quality control, and manufacturing techniques. The article also describes plant organization, auto parts management, workforce administration, and the NUMMI's "team" concept.

480. "Nissan motor: Nissan announces organizational changes." Business Japan. (April 1990): 23-24.

Various organizational changes were implemented at Nissan Motor Co. Ltd. on January 1 of 1990: 1) strengthening of global planning capabilities, 2) establishment of a new Corporate Customer Satisfaction (CCS) Promotion office, 3) establishment of a new Environmental and Safety Engineering Department, 4) creation of a new Electronic Engineering Division, and 5) reinforcement of the regional sales system. These changes are designed to build a stronger organization by creating new departments and restructuring and consolidating existing ones.

481. Pollack, Andrew. "Isuzu to stop manufacturing passenger cars." New York Times. (December 20, 1992): 6.

As a result of Japan's severe economic slump, Isuzu Motors Ltd. announced its plan to stop producing passenger cars in the U.S. and refocus its manufacturing techniques on trucks, recreational vehicles and diesel engines. Isuzu's decision reduced the number of Japanese car manufacturers to eight.

482. Pollack, Andrew. "Mazda drops luxury line plan for U.S." New York Times. (October 27, 1992): D1, D9.

With an economic downturn both at home and abroad, and a projected decline of nearly 65% in profits for the 1992 fiscal year, Mazda Motor Corp. announced its plan to drop its Amati models from the U.S. luxury market. The company also announced significant cutbacks in auto racing and would redirect its resources to focus on product development, emission control, and auto safety issues.

483. Rae, John B. Nissan/Datsun: a history of Nissan Motor Corporation in U.S.A., 1960-1980. New York, NY: McGraw-Hill Book Co., 1982.

This book provides the history of Nissan Motor Corp. and describes the impact of their cars and trucks on the U.S. market. The following key elements are their secrets to success which were discussed in this volume: dealer and marketing organizations; parts, service, and engineering groups; transportation and distribution systems; and administrative organization. Besides the internal strategies, this book also explains how Nissan analyzed the impact of the Arab oil embargo and the energy crisis and reacted in their product designs.

484. Rescigno, Richard. "At the crossroads: Subaru strives to
     get back into gear." Barron's. 68.13 (March 28, 1988):
     15, 37-40.

     Records the financial difficulties of Subaru of America
     Inc., the U.S. distributor of Fuji Heavy Industries. The
     company lost $30 million in the fiscal year ending in
     October 1987.   This loss, the first loss in over a
     decade, was due to the rising value of the yen, severe
     sales competition, and decreased demand.   Subaru is
     offering rebates to attract customers for the time being.
     Its long-term marketing plan is based on new product
     development, especially upscale models to be produced in
     the United States with Isuzu Motors. The goal is to sell
     260,000-300,000 cars annually by 1992.

485. Rescigno, Richard.   "Here comes Honda: it's now no. 4
     among U.S. car makers...and pushing." Barron's.   65.48
     (December 2, 1985): 48-49.

     Mr. Tetsuo Chino, the President of Honda of America,
     offers his views on the role and prospects of his company
     in a personal interview with reporters from Barron's. As
     the number four auto producer in America, Honda has
     ambitious goals for the future.   The company plans to
     increase up to 60% content of American-made parts on its
     U.S.-produced cars. Auto production in the Marysville,
     Ohio, plant will increase. Honda's ultimate goal is to
     Americanize its production, capital, and management in
     order to be accepted as an American corporation.

486. Sakiya, Tetsuo.   Honda motor: the man, the management,
     the machines.   Tokyo ; New York, NY: Kodansha
     International Ltd., 1982.

     This book addresses three main topics: 1) a detailed
     description of Mr. Soichiro Honda and Mr. Takeo Fujisawa
     who are the driving forces behind Honda's success; 2) an
     in-depth analysis of Honda Motor's corporate management
     and strategies from the view of Japan's cultural
     traditions and the radical political, economic and
     sociological changes the country has undergone during the
     past century; and 3) Honda Motor's history following the
     retirement of its co-founders.

487. Schreffler, Roger.   "A decade of progress: Honda moves
     ever closer to its goal of designing, engineering and
     manufacturing cars in the U.S."   Chilton's Automotive
     Industries. 172.11 (November 1992): 46-49.

     Honda of America Manufacturing Inc., the first
     Japanese-built automobile company in the United States,
     is now reaching a decade of progress. Although Honda was
     first started as a motorcycle plant, the company's unique
     management strategies and rapid development have made its
     first Accord model America's best-selling car for the
     past three years. The company now sells its products in
     17 countries, including Canada.   Through a decade of
     growth, Japanese investment in America has grown to over

2.7 million cars and light trucks per year. This article
includes detailed description of the Honda plant in
Marysville, Ohio, including the plant's operations,
engineering, designing, manufacturing and management
strategies.

488. Shimizu, Yoshihiko.   "Toyota Motor buckles down to
overtake GM."   _Tokyo Business Today_.   59.2 (February
1991): 32-34.

Toyota Motor Corp. delivered its domestic and overseas
production and sales plans, targeted on 1995.   The plan
includes a comprehensive R&D and management programs,
extensive studies of location policies, labor and capital
management. Toyota's strength and confidence in the U.S.
production base was further expanded through its joint
venture with General Motors to establish New United Motor
Manufacturing Inc. (NUMMI) in California, which began
operation in December 1984.   The NUMMI joint venture
contract with GM will expire in 1996.   Toyota plans to
expand its own production base in the United States.

489. Shimizu, Yoshihiko and David Williams.   "Rusty guns
threaten Toyota's grip on top slot."   _Tokyo Business
Today_.   (August 1989): 14-19.

Toyota Motor Corp., Japan's largest auto manufacturer and
the model of the country's top mass production and
marketing, is beginning to show signs of decay.   The
major factor is the competitive pressure and increasing
industrial power of the number two Japanese automaker,
Nissan Motor Co.   Market share and corporate morale are
the elements the company is concentrating on.   Toyota
also adds "internationalization" as the third strategic
focus.   Having established an auto production base
successfully in the U.S., Toyota has launched a similar
effort in the European auto market.   Toyota hopes to
revive its corporate image and marketing strategies
during the 1990s.

490. Shook, Robert L.   _Honda: an American success story_.   New
York, NY: Prentice Hall, 1988.

Honda, the world's leading motorcycle producer as well as
the first Japanese company to manufacture automobiles in
the United States, is discussed in this book.   During the
1980s, while United States industry was searching for
excellence, the quality of American-made Honda was no
doubt the superb example among automobile manufacturers
in the U.S.   This book analyzes Honda's managerial
innovations, highly motivated and inspired workforce, and
the company's developmental processes.

491. Smith, Charles.   "Newly listed Mitsubishi Motors pins
sales hopes on Japanese market."   _Far Eastern Economic
Review_.   143.3 (January 19, 1989): 60-61.

The recent market strategy for the Mitsubishi Motors

Corp. (MMC) is to strengthen its dealer network,
particularly in fast growing residential areas. MMC will
also focus on developing a new medium-sized car and on
strengthening the 2,000 c.c. sector, currently the
fastest growing area in the domestic market. The key
weakness of MMC's financial strength is the company's
negative balances of net interest earnings on loans and
investments. The strategy of offering a full range of
vehicles rather than aiming at one market segment also
hurts profitability.

492. Smith, Charles. "Nissan finds new fight to hold its
ground: new look, new life." Far Eastern Economic
Review. 141.28 (July 14, 1988): 68-70.

Nissan Motor Co. experienced the biggest turnaround among
Japanese companies in the 1980s. New personnel
management, new model designs, and new marketing and
sales strategies have been underway since the appointment
of the new president, Yutaka Kume, in July 1985. Kume
encourages major input on model design from younger
people in the company. Under Kume's new management,
Nissan is now exhibiting a new fresh look. The next
challenge is to show the company's sales power and design
improvement through consumers' reactions.

493. Snowdon, Mark. "Austin Rover: the joint venture with
Honda." International Journal of Technology Management.
2.1 (1987): 67-73.

The joint venture between Austin Rover and Honda Motor
Company in 1979 is described in this paper. The venture
has been a success because both sides were prepared to
adopt principles designed to maintain a stable balanced
relationship and each has worked to try to put them into
practice. One project resulting from the partnership is
the XX Design and Development Agreement, where the two
sides each provided a product development team to work
jointly on designing a new car. Due to the big success
in this project, more collaboration and joint programs
are planned in the future.

494. Snyder, Jesse. "Subaru drives into new niches."
Advertising Age. 57.35 (June 16, 1986): S33-S34.

Subaru of America has been exploring markets other
importers have ignored by using low-key advertising. The
announcement that Isuzu Motors and Fuji Heavy Industries
would build an assembly plant in the U.S. suggests that
Subaru is being affected by growing competition and trade
issues. The company sells more than 150,000 cars a year
and is planning to build a retail network capable of
selling 250,000 to 300,000 units annually. Its market
strategy includes establishing a stronger dealer network,
insuring customer satisfaction, and promoting high-key
advertising.

495. Stack, Bill. "Toyota in Bluegrass country." Industry
Week. 238.11 (June 5, 1989): 30-33.

When Toyota officials first announced their site selection in Georgetown, Kentucky, in December 1985, local residents had mixed feelings of hope and anxiety. Building the plant in Georgetown meant providing over 3,000 jobs for the local towns' people, but the fear of outside influences on the closely-knit community preoccupied the Georgetown residents. Open, two-way communications between the Kentucky state and local communities, as well as with Toyota, helped to alleviate the cultural and social barriers faced by these two countries.

496. Sugiura, Hideo. "How Honda localizes its global strategy." Sloan Management Review. 32.1 (Fall 1990): 77-82.

This article was written by the retired chairman of Honda Motor Co. He describes Honda's successful localization strategy, discusses the company's early experiments in international management, and analyzes the implementation of these corporate philosophies and their functions based on his decades of practical experience with the company. Honda promotes internationalization as its overseas strategy, with major emphasis on the localization of products, profits, production, and management. In the firm's Ohio auto plant, Honda stresses the importance of three policies: 1) establishing good human relations between the management and the workforce, 2) maintaining and promoting harmony with the local community, and 3) giving top priority to maintaining high quality standards in its products.

497. Tanzen, Andrew and Marc Beauchamp. "Confession time at Nissan." Forbes. 138.10 (November 3, 1986): 48-51.

This paper is a case study of Nissan Motor Co. Ltd., Japan's second largest automobile producer. In recent years, business at Nissan has dropped significantly, and the company reported an operating loss in 1986. There are three major problems that the company is currently facing: 1) a shrinking share of the domestic market, 2) an inefficient Japanese dealer system, and 3) a troubled overseas production strategy. The company needs to overcome these problems in order to move ahead in the competitive automobile industry and trade.

498. Taylor, Alex III. "Nissan Motor Corp. in U.S.A.: driving for the market's heart." Fortune. 125.12 (June 15, 1992): 120-21.

Since 1985 Nissan's American sales of cars and trucks have slipped 30%. There are many reasons to explain the market crunch: a lack of strong products in the central model lineup, confusing shifts in marketing and advertising, and unstable dealer-manufacturer relationships. Nissan's executives are planning to launch three new vehicles--the minivan Quest, the Infiniti J30 sports sedan, and the stylish Altima--as the first corrective step to solve these problems.

499. Taylor, Alex III. "Nissan's bold bid for market share."
     <u>Fortune</u>. 121.1 (January 1, 1990): 99-101.

     Nissan's auto sales rose about 7% in 1989, more than any
     other major automaker, and its debut of the Infiniti Q45
     further enhanced Nissan's image as Japan's high-fashion
     automaker. The company expects to boost U.S. car and
     truck sales around 20%, from 670,000 in 1989 to 800,000
     by 1992 or 1993. Success in the U. S. auto market is
     difficult to achieve. Nissan's continuous effort on
     design and investment has stirred competitiveness in
     Honda and Toyota. The company may have to depend on its
     current successful models until its new line of family
     sedans catches on.

500. Taylor, Alex III. "Why Toyota keeps getting better and
     better and better."   <u>Fortune</u>.   122.13 (November 19,
     1990): 66-79.

     During the 1990 model year, Toyota sold more than one
     million automobiles and trucks in the United States. By
     introducing six all-new vehicles within 14 months, Toyota
     has grabbed a 43% share of car sales in Japan. Another
     six new models are due in the United States in the next
     12 months. The company is superior in quality,
     production, and efficiency. Constant improvement is the
     key. The "kanban," or, the "just-in-time" system which
     was initiated in the early 1980s, is the key for Toyota
     in speeding up its entire production process. The system
     aims to manufacture only what is needed, when it is
     needed, and in the quantity needed. Globalization is the
     company's goal. Toyota is tightening its grip on
     Southeast Asia, making inroads in Latin America, and
     mobilizing for an assault on Europe. Long number three
     among the world's automakers, Toyota could push ahead of
     Ford in car sales in 1993.

501. "Toyota makes full model changes in Camry and Vista."
     <u>Business Japan</u>. 35.10 (October 1990): 14-21.

     Records the recent full model changes of Toyota Motor
     Corporation's Camry and Vista series. There are three
     major areas of development: 1) creation of sophisticated
     and dynamic styling; 2) provision of a safe, spacious and
     comfortable cabin; and 3) improvements in the engine,
     chassis, and body to achieve superior performance and
     economy. The production, domestic registration, export,
     and overseas production results from January to June 1990
     period are also included in this article.

502. "Toyota motor: Toyota's worldwide sales drop in fiscal
     1992." <u>Japan 21st</u>. (May 1992): 18-20.

     For fiscal year 1992, Toyota Motor Corp.'s worldwide
     vehicle sales were down 1.2% or about 25,000 units
     compared with the same period in the previous year.
     Several major factors could explain the company's decline
     in earnings: exchange rates, depreciation costs and
     personnel, marketing, and other administrative expenses.

The company is optimistic about the domestic market, but the possibility of a recovery of global market conditions still looks dim.

503. Treece, James B. "Subaru gets out of the fast lane." Business Week. 3008 (July 20, 1987): 112F-G.

After enjoying years of rising profits, business at Subaru of America, Inc. fell sharply due to the following reasons: the strong yen, marketing mistakes, and management's failure to identify the firm's limits. One major mistake has been a move towards more expensive cars such as the XT Sports Car featuring four-wheel drive. The timing of such a move was very inappropriate as the yen's value soared. Subaru is now moving back into the subcompact field which at one time earned big profits. Its joint venture with Fuji Heavy Industries seems not too smooth because of administrative problems and predicted over-production of smaller cars in the United States.

504. Vasilash, Gary S. "Designing the car of the decade." Production. 102.4 (April 1990): 54-56.

Mazda Motor Corp.'s MX-5 Miata is considered by many auto experts as the most important car to come out of Japan in the 1980s. Its front-engine, rear-wheel-drive design, with a relatively light weight (2,182 pounds) and low cost (a sticker price of $13,800), attracts buyers worldwide. Mazda's "flexible production" is the primary reason for the company's high profit gains. Although computer-generated images and simulation techniques could automate and speed up the entire designing process, Mazda insisted on combining full-scale clay models and drawings with a computer to design the Miata.

505. Vasilash, Gary S. "U.S. CMM helps assure the quality of the Lexus engine." Production. 101.9 (September 1989): 102-04.

With the help of Brown & Sharpe Manufacturing Co.'s Process Control Robots (PCR) Model 1057, Toyota Motor Corp. is able to assure the quality of its Lexus engines. The PCR is located at the end of what is considered to be one of the world's most advanced flexible machining lines, the so-called Coordinate Measuring Machine (CMM).

506. Yasuda, Yuzo. 40 years, 20 million ideas: the Toyota suggestion system. Cambridge, MA: Productivity Press, Inc., 1991.

This book describes the major concept of the Toyota Creative Idea suggestion system designed by the late Taicchi Ohno. The system was based on the principles of "just-in-time" and automation. The major goal of the system is not to save or make lots of money, but to involve the workers in improving the management of the company. The book is divided into five chapters. Chapter one describes the theory of the system and the

organizational structure that supports it. Chapter two
traces the origins of the system--an idea that came from
the Ford River Rouge plant in 1949 and was transformed
into a system adopted by the Toyota automobile factories.
The history and methods of the Good Idea (GI) Club, a
unique group that originated from an ad hoc social
gathering of Toyota's top suggestion writers, are
described in chapter three. Chapter four records ten
examples of suggestions submitted from the different
departments in the company. The last chapter concludes
with comments on the system and makes important
suggestions for companies that plan to adopt Toyota's
theories.

Part II

PERIODICALS, REFERENCES, AND AUDIO-VISUAL AIDS

8

Periodicals

507. <u>Automobile International</u>.   New York, NY: McGraw-Hill, 19uu-.   Monthly.

Covering current developments in equipment and techniques for the automotive service industries, this magazine is geared to domestic and foreign car specialists.

508. <u>Automobile Quarterly</u>.   Princeton,   NJ: Automobile Quarterly Inc., 1962-.   Quarterly.

This periodical carries many worldwide feature articles with major emphasis on sports cars and high performance vehicles.   Excellent color photo reproduction and high quality printing make this magazine quite distinctive. Updates of Japanese sports cars and current new models are frequently covered in this periodical.

509. <u>Automotive News</u>.   Detroit,   MI: Automotive   News Circulation Dept., 1925-.   Semi-weekly.

This newspaper deals with broad subject areas of the American as well as Japanese automotive industries, including auto research and development, the introduction of new products, sales volumes of major automotive corporations, statistics of auto production and sales, government legislations affecting the auto industry, auction directory of all the states, and classified lists of auto trade sales and dealerships.

510. <u>Autoweek</u>. Chicago, IL: Leon Mandel, 1958-. Weekly.

Published in newspaper format and devoted exclusively to auto racing, this weekly journal focuses on the world car industry, with introduction and description of Japanese, American, and European auto vehicles, including sports sedans, and performance and sports cars.   It includes extensive coverage of the international Grand Prix Formula One and stock car races. Lists of upcoming races are covered in each issue.

511. Business Week. New York, NY: McGraw Hill, 1929-. Weekly.

The magazine provides international business information, global economic analysis, corporation news, finance, science and technology trends, speeches of successful business executives, and so on. Some issues put significant emphasis on the Japanese automotive industry with subjects ranging from economic and social aspects to environmental concerns, marketing and technological innovations.

512. Car and Driver. New York, NY: Hachette Magazines, Inc., 1955-. Monthly.

This popular auto magazine covers descriptions of American, Japanese and European sports cars. It contains several "road-tests" articles describing the cars' history, performance, and lineage. Major subjects include specifications on the engine, capacities and dimensions, interior design, brakes, steering, wheels, and tires. Each issue contains several articles on sports car racing and automobile engineering.

513. Chilton's Automotive Industries. Radnor, PA: Chilton Co., 1976-. Semi-monthly except monthly in April, July and December. (Continues: Automotive industries).

This journal is devoted exclusively to articles on automotive business and trade. Updated news on government legislation, reports on current European and Japanese auto markets, and stock reports appear regularly in each issue. The magazine covers such topics as engineering, production, design, new products, electronics, market share, as well as the industrial outlook.

514. Four Wheeler. Canoga Park, CA: Four Wheeler Pub. Co., 1962-. Monthly.

One of the most popular magazines on four-wheel-drive vehicles of American, Japanese, or European manufacturers, this journal contains several feature articles on racing, touring, personal interviews with experts in the field, new model designs, and maintenance and repair. The "Four wheeler of the year" is a special column intended for current buyers with information provided for one specific model on prices and options, specifications, and performance ratings.

515. Industry Week. Cleveland, OH: Penton Publishing, 1970-. Bi-weekly.

This journal covers feature articles, news items, and recent releases aimed at executives' activities in the

area of industrial management. It contains current news
of the business world; automation in technology and
business fields; management strategies of major U.S.,
Japanese, and European companies; automotive trends and
analysis of the U.S. and Japanese auto companies; and
worldwide economic outlook.

516. <u>International Motor Business</u>. London: The Economist
Intelligence Unit, 1985-. Tri-monthly.

Severe competition has made the motor industry
transnational. Auto manufacturers are looking further in
search of low-cost suppliers, and the entire industry is
gradually being linked by the growing demand for joint
ventures. This journal provides overview and detail for
understanding these emerging trends and their
consequences. Each issue contains an "Industry review"
which examines the current trends of the motor industry
and market. "Three other research-based reports" cover
materials ranging from the auto sector of a particular
country to a company's profile. "Worldwide automotive
trends" examines vehicle production and sales with
forecasts for the succeeding years. Topics relating to
the Japanese automobile industry are frequently discussed
in this periodical.

517. <u>The JAMA Forum</u>. Tokyo, Japan: Japan Automobile
Manufacturers Association, 1982-. Quarterly.

This journal, published quarterly by the Japan Automobile
Manufacturers Association, provides not only Japan's auto
news but also America's technological trends in the auto
field. It covers issues on bilateral auto trade and
offers specific details of the U.S. and Japanese auto
companies, including production volumes, market shares,
import and export statistics, and future perspectives.

518. <u>Japan 21st</u>. [Tokyo: Nihon Kogyo Shinbun], 1992-.
Monthly. (Continues: <u>Business Japan</u>).

This monthly publication carries reports and essays
centered on industrial and economic developments in
Japan, as well as on the political and cultural sectors.
Each issue consists of regular columns on Japan today
(recent news on Japanese economic and industrial
development); business trends (updated automobile
developments of Nissan, Toyota, Honda, Mazda, Mitsubishi,
Isuzu, and other electronic news and reports);
corporation news; Tokyo reports (personal interviews with
business managers and top company presidents from
domestic as well as foreign countries); plus a special
report column focused on one major topic for each volume,
such as: environmental problems, nuclear power
generation, future business trends, and science and
technology developments.

519. <u>Japan Automotive News</u>. Tokyo, Japan: Automotive Herald
Co., Ltd., 19uu-. Monthly.

Published monthly, this pamphlet covers facts and figures
of the Japanese automobile industry.   It is a basic
source   for   the   latest   Japanese   auto   trends   and
statistics.

520. **Japan Company Handbook**. Tokyo, Japan: Toyo Keizai Inc.,
     1974-. Quarterly.

This handbook provides the latest financial information
on all Japanese corporations listed on the Tokyo, Osaka,
and Nagoya stock exchanges with special reference to
their   past   records,   present   showings,   and   future
possibilities.   Each issue covers approximately 1,200
companies. Under the section "automobiles & trucks", it
includes   about   30   companies,   including   automakers,
manufacturers,   auto   body   assemblers,   electrical   or
hydraulic equipment makers, and makers of mufflers or
mechanical   components   for   car   interiors.   This
comprehensive   volume   is   a   primary   source   for   the
understanding of the Japanese industrial and business
fields.

521. **Japan Economic Review**. Tokyo, Japan: The Japan Economic
     Review, Ltd., 1969-. Monthly.

A monthly review of business and economic news in Japan,
this magazine puts major emphasis on auto exports.   It
contains regular columns on automobiles, electronics, and
manufacturers   and   discusses   the   impact   of   foreign
countries on the Japanese economy.

522. **Japan Report**. New York, NY: Japan Information Center,
     1955-. Semi-monthly.

This newsletter was issued in Washington by the Embassy
of Japan from August 1955-57, and then continued by the
Consulate General of Japan and its Information Center in
New York.   The major emphasis is on the current economic
and political events of the country and of Asia as a
whole.   The automobile industry as the leading industry
in Japan is frequently cited in this newsletter.

523. **Japan Times**. Japan: Japan Times and Advertiser, 1940-.
     Covers the latest trends, news, and updates on Japanese
     trade, business, politics, and reports the current status
     of the Japanese automobile industry and international
     auto trade.

524. **Japanese Motor Business**. London: Economic Intelligence
     Unit, 1984-. Tri-monthly.

This journal traces Japan's fast-expanding production
base across the world and the new trade alliances and
financial flows which are emerging.   Each issue contains
feature articles on manufacturing techniques of key
Japanese plants, Japanese management and marketing
practices, Japanese automobile and component producers,
and statistics of Japanese vehicle production, sales,
exports, and forecasts.

525. JETRO Monitor.   New York, NY: Japan External Trade
     Organization, 19uu-. Monthly.

     A monthly newsletter published by the Japan External
     Trade Organization, this journal puts major focus on
     Japanese economic and trade issues. It includes Japanese
     financial trade figures and statistics, news briefs of
     recent Japanese corporate developments, and announcements
     of trade-related conferences and seminars.

526. Motor Trend. Los Angeles, CA: Petersen Publishing Co.,
     1949-. Monthly.

     This is one of the best public-interest automobile
     journals in the United States. It covers automobiles
     produced by Japan, United States, and Europe. Feature
     articles describe the newly designed models and
     automotive industry trends. Several extensive road tests
     in each issue offer detailed performance data together
     with various pictures of each car tested.   Driving
     impressions, consumer surveys, long-term tests, and auto
     companies' reports are found in every issue. This title
     is also popular for its prized "Car of the Year" award.

527. Road & Track. Newport Beach, CA: CBS Publishing Co.,
     1947-. Monthly.

     This popular auto magazine covers all types of
     international automobiles with major emphasis on sports
     and performance autos. Several road tests in each issue
     provide details on performance and mechanical
     specifications along with pictures of each car tested.
     Feature articles describe various sports/performance
     autos, auto racing, and new models of the year.

528. Tokyo Business Today. Tokyo, Japan: Toyo Keizai Inc.,
     1986-. Monthly.

     This news magazine covers Japanese economics, business,
     and industries in particular, and science and technology
     in general. Each issue includes a cover story of recent
     popular concern, such as the oil crisis, foreign firms'
     investments in Japan, or banking development; a feature
     column on recent Japanese business trends; the impact of
     the economic recession on domestic firms; automobile
     development; news of the recent collaboration of
     automotive companies; industry updates on major Japanese
     companies; and regular speeches given by prominent
     Japanese scholars or top company officials on
     business-related topics.

529. Ward's Auto World. Detroit, MI: Ward's Communications,
     Inc., 1969-. Monthly.

     The magazine covers a widerange of materials on the
     automobile industry. Topics include recent automobile
     developments, business trends, dealership, quality
     control, assembly line production, Japanese-owned U.S.
     transplants, market trends, industry forecasts, and so

on. It also reports the developments of major automotive
corporations,   their   personnel   changes,   recent
innovations, managerial skills, and technological trends.

530. The Wheel Extended: A Toyota Quarterly Review. Tokyo,
Japan: Toyota Motor Corporation, 1971-. Quarterly.

This   publication   includes   articles   on   Japanese
transportation systems, automobile industry and trade,
and auto-related current awareness programs, such as
traffic   control   in   high-density   urban   areas,   air
pollution cause by exhaust fumes, government regulations
of public safety and health, and so on.   Each issue
contains four to six articles dealing with auto-related
topics. It is extensively illustrated with maps, photos,
and statistical tables.

9

Bibliographies

531. Boger, Karl. <u>Japan's direct foreign investment: an annotated bibliography</u>. New York, NY: Greenwood Press, 1989.

This book provides a list of 673 bibliographical citations for materials written in the English language, and mainly addresses the issue of Japanese overseas investments from a U.S. perspective. Content arrangement is according to the geographical distribution of Japan's foreign investments. It includes North and South America, Europe, Africa, Asia, and the Pacific Ocean Region. A great amount of information was identified on the United States and Southeast Asia since Japanese investments have been concentrated heavily in these areas. Japanese investment in the U.S. automobile industry is also covered.

532. Boger, Karl. <u>Postwar industrial policy in Japan: an annotated bibliography</u>. Metuchen, NJ: The Scarecrow Press, 1988.

Providing over 500 bibliographical entries about Japanese industrial policy in the postwar era, this book emphasizes the issue of industrial policy from a U.S. perspective. It provides an extensive context for understanding how Japanese industrial policy works and how it has influenced economic growth in Japan. This volume includes materials in the English language only, with discussions of the Japanese automobile industry from the industrial and managerial points of view, and on the United States' and Japan's economic relations.

533. Dunphy, Dexter C. and Bruce W. Stening. <u>Japan organization behavior and management: an annotated bibliography</u>. Hong Kong: Asian Research Service, 1984.

This annotated bibliography provides a broad selection of
journals and monographs in English from 1970 to 1983,
with subjects ranging from Japanese employment practices,
decision-making, workers' attitudes, management style,
and organizational structure.   Although it does not
directly touch upon Japan's automobile industry, the book
does provide a basic organizational structure and
managerial style applied by the Japanese industrial and
business fields.

534. Keresztesi, Michael and Gary R. Cocozzoli.   Japan's
economic challenge: a bibliographic sourcebook.   New
York, NY: Garland Publishing, 1988.

This bibliography includes more than 3,000 citations in
English, with subjects including Japanese historical and
cultural developments; foreign economic relations;
industrial policies; domestic trade and trade relations
with other foreign countries; labor, social policy,
employment, and women's status in economic settings; and
operations, structures, and strategies of business
organizations and corporations. The bibliography touches
upon Japanese auto-related issues, including corporate
management, quality control, and research & development.
Materials range from the late 1970s to mid-1987.

535. Lee, Molly Kyung Sook Chang.   East Asian economics: a
guide to information sources.   Detroit, MI: Gale Research
Company, 1979.

This annotated bibliographical source brings to readers
a wide selection of materials in English concerning the
economics of China, Japan, Korea, and Taiwan from 1900 to
1979.   While the chapter on Japan does not directly deal
with the automobile industry itself, it does provide the
basics of Japanese economic history and industrial
development; technological innovations; economic planning
and growth; international economics and trade; and
labor-management relations.

10

Encyclopedias

536. Davis, G. J. <u>Automotive reference: a new approach to the world of auto-related information</u>. Boise, Idaho: Whitehorse, 1987.

This dictionary provides the most comprehensive worldwide information on the auto industry field. It is one unique source for a variety of purposes. The Automotive reference covers information on auto repairing, auto racing, auto services, car advertising, driver education, car products, auto manufacturers, auto-related publications, and so forth. Japanese automobile companies, company histories and development, car models and designs, transplanted operations in the United States, and the auto parts and components industries are covered in this volume.

537. Georgano, G. N., ed. <u>The New encyclopedia of motorcars: 1885 to the present</u>. New York, NY: E.P. Dutton, 1982.

This encyclopedia contains over 230 types of motorcars available on the world auto market, dated 1885 to 1982. Only those cars which were built for private use as passenger-carrying vehicles are included. A complete history is given for each new car type with photos of various models from earliest to present. The leading Japanese auto manufacturers, including Toyota, Honda, Mazda, Isuzu, Nissan, and Mitsubishi, are covered in this encyclopedia.

538. <u>Goodheart-Willcox automotive encyclopedia</u>. South Holland, IL: Goodheart-Willcox Co., 1983.

This encyclopedia covers fundamental principles involved in vehicle operation for all types of cars available on the market. It contains construction details, principles of operation, latest mechanical processes and basic

service procedures.   The volume includes detailed
information on the fundamentals of electricity,
hydraulics, pneumatics, internal combustion, and exhaust
emission control.

539. The World of automobiles: an illustrated encyclopedia of
the motor car. Milwaukee, WI: Purnell Reference Books,
1977, 22 vols.

This comprehensive twenty-two volume set contains major
sections on international automobile history,
fundamentals of engine designs, who's who in the world
motor industry and the world of speed in auto-racing and
sports cars activities. The entire set is fully
illustrated with photo reproductions collected throughout
the world and detailed drawings of car engines.

11

Yearbooks

540. <u>The Automobile industry, Japan and Toyota</u>. Aichi, Japan: Toyota Motor Corporation, 1983-. Annual. (Continues: <u>Motor industry of Japan</u>).

This annual report covers an overview of the Toyota Motor Corp., the statistics of its local and overseas production, new registrations for both domestic and imported cars, and imports and exports of Japanese motor vehicles. The report is illustrated chiefly, with charts and tables. It is a comprehensive statistical source for the Japanese auto industry and the Toyota Motor Corp.

541. <u>Automotive News Market Data Book</u>. Detroit, MI: Automotive News, 1976-. Annual.

The following statistics are provided in each annual publication: worldwide vehicle and truck productions; global car and truck sales and registrations; products and specifications of new models on passenger cars and light-duty trucks; the retail prices of the domestic and imported vehicles; car options and equipment on U.S. models of the year; America's major auto dealers arranged by franchise; a special section of "Who's who in the auto industry"; and directories of automobile and dealers associations worldwide. This magazine includes comprehensive statistical data and company updates of both the Japanese and American auto industries.

542. <u>Facts and info: guide to Japan's auto parts industry</u>. [s.l.]: Automotive Herald Co., Ltd., 19uu-. Annual.

Released annually, this handy guide contains information related to the Japanese auto parts industry, including current trends, company updates, market potential, and production figures.

543. Gillis, Jack. The car book. New York: Harper & Row,
     1981-. Annual.

     This book is a consumer guide for both domestic and
     foreign cars. Published annually, the book is based on
     data collected and developed by private automobile
     engineering firms, the U.S. Department of Transportation,
     and the Center for Auto Safety. It includes chapters on
     auto purchasing, car safety, fuel economy, car
     maintenance, auto warranty, auto insurance, and used car
     purchasing. Each chapter contains primarily charts and
     figures of automobile ratings to help consumers make the
     best choice based on the statistics and data compiled in
     this book.

544. Guide to the Motor Industry of Japan. Tokyo: Japan Motor
     Industrial Federation, 1960-. Annual.

     There are five major sections in this guide: 1)
     description of major Japanese automobile manufacturers,
     including Daihatsu, Fuji, Honda, Isuzu, Mazda,
     Mitsubishi, Nissan, Suzuki, and Toyota; 2) fully
     illustrated catalogue of Japanese passenger car models,
     commercial vehicles, and motorcycles; 3) specifications
     on engines, transmissions, brakes, steering, suspension,
     axles, and tires; 4) motor vehicle statistics on
     production, export, and registrations; and 5) directory
     of organizations and manufacturers.

545. Japan autotech report: year book. Tokyo, Japan: AI
     Technical Research Associates, 1986-. Annual.

     Based on product design and auto construction
     technologies, Japan autotech report explores many areas
     of research interests ranging from automation on product
     design to technological advancement in auto-related
     experiments.

546. Mazda Motor Corporation Annual Report. Hiroshima, Japan:
     Mazda Motor Corp., 19uu-. Annual.

     Published by Mazda Motor Corp., this annual report
     contains detailed information about the company's
     production, imports, exports, market shares, auto safety
     measures, and descriptions of employee job security and
     work environment.

547. Mitsubishi Motors Facts & Figures. Tokyo, Japan:
     Mitsubishi Motors, 198u-. Annual. (Continues:
     Mitsubishi Motors Fact Book).

     Published annually, this yearbook contains statistical
     data and texts of the Mitsubishi Motors Corp., including
     market shares, production volumes, imports, and exports.

548. Motor Vehicle Statistics of Japan. Tokyo, Japan: Japan
     Automobile Manufacturers Association, 19uu-. Annual.

     Records the statistics of Japanese motor vehicles for the

past thirty years. It contains extensive figures of
motor vehicles in use, new registrations, production,
imports, exports, and a section on motorcycles and motor
scooters.

549. **MVMA Motor Vehicle Facts & Figures**. Detroit, MI: Motor
Vehicle Manufacturers Association of the United States,
Inc., 1978-. Annual.

This publication provides detailed information on the
international automobile industry in statistical format.
It includes chapters on auto production, sales and
registration; car ownership and purpose of usage;
economic and social impact on consumer expenditures, fuel
economy, employment rates; and pollution control
expenditures, taxes, and regulations.

550. **Standard Trade Index of Japan**. [Tokyo]: Japan Chamber of
Commerce and Industry, 1958-. Annual.

For promotion of Japan's international trade, the Japan
Chamber of Commerce and Industry, the Ministry of
International Trade and Industry, and 489 local Chambers
of Commerce and Industry throughout the country have
published this book since 1957. The directory contains
precise information on Japanese industrial products and
all other marketable products. Company profiles of major
Japanese automobile industries are also included in this
directory.

551. **Toyota Information Handbook**. Tokyo, Japan: Toyota Motor
Sales Co., Ltd., 1980-. Annual.

This handbook contains basic facts and figures on Toyota.
It includes descriptions and statistics for the
organization of the company, its automotive and
non-automotive products, production system, marketing
strategies, domestic and export sale records, research
and development, employees' activities, and a financial
review. Each issue covers annual trade statistics for
the previous year.

552. **Ward's Automotive Yearbook**. Detroit, MI: Ward's
Communications, 1938-. Annual.

There are three main parts in this yearbook:
technological trends, the global auto industry, and the
U.S. auto industry. The first part emphasizes car
production, imports, exports, governmental issues
concerning federal regulation of emission standards, car
prices, marketing, consumer information, and so on. The
second part includes the world overview of the auto
industry in the following geographic areas:
Asia/Pacific, Europe, South America, and North America.
Within each country, it includes: a list of automakers
for that nation, the monthly statistics of vehicle
production, new registrations, projections of exports and
imports for the next two years, and the analysis of
market shares shown by pie charts. The third part covers

in detail the statistics, new models/designs, market
shares, import/export data, and articles exclusively for
the U.S. auto industry.

553. World Automotive Industry. New York, NY: Automotive
International, 19uu-. Annual.

This annual publication provides worldwide automotive
market information. Each issue includes a summary of
vehicle production for the previous year, vehicle
productions of 34 foreign countries, a list of top-ten
vehicle-producing nations for the preceding year,
statistics of worldwide vehicle registrations, U.S.
exports of automotive parts for the past five years, and
world trade of cars and trucks. It is fully illustrated
with charts and tables.

554. World Automotive Market. New York, NY: Automobile
International, 1956-. Annual.

This volume is the product of Automobile International's
annual worldwide survey compiled primarily from
statistics and estimates of the Society of Motor
Manufacturers and Traders Ltd. of London, the
International Road Federation, and the research staff of
Automobile International. Each issue contains the
following statistical figures for the preceding year:
vehicle production of 30 countries; vehicle registrations
worldwide; models of cars and trucks in 24 countries;
world map of vehicles on the road; vehicle exports to 141
countries from 9 major producing countries; and the U.S.
exports of automotive products arranged by country of
designation.

555. World Cars. Pelham, NY: Herald Books, 1972-. Annual.

A comprehensive volume that covers auto-related
information throughout the world, this yearbook provides
specifications on engine, transmission, performance,
brakes, electrical equipment, dimensions and weight for
each car model. The whole volume is geographically
arranged and fully illustrated. The world car
manufactures and coachbuilders are outlined with
descriptions of their history, structure, and activities.

556. World Motor Vehicle Data. Detroit, MI: Motor Vehicle
Manufacturers Association of the United States, 19uu-.
Annual.

The data in this report are supplied by foreign
government agencies, trade associations, private services
and the press. It contains a statistical compilation of
international motor vehicle data covering production
totals by manufacturers as well as by country.

12

Other Reference Works

557. Carroll, William. <u>Bill Carroll's automotive troubleshooting glossary</u>. San Marcos, CA: Auto Book Press, 1973.

This manual provides an extensive glossary of automotive terminologies commonly used by auto mechanics, engineers and auto enthusiasts.

558. Coster, Jean de. <u>Dictionary for automotive engineering: English, French, German</u>. New York, NY: K. G. Saur, 1990.

Written in three different languages, this dictionary covers the following major areas of automotive engineering: engine, chassis, transmission, steering, braking system, fuel system, lubricants, electrical system, and workshop equipment. With major focus on the electronic ignition systems, an area of significant importance in the automotive engineering field, this dictionary provides a complete listing of nearly 900 terms most commonly used in the automotive engineering field. The dictionary is a good resource for both domestic and foreign cars.

559. Goodsell, Don. <u>Dictionary of automotive engineering</u>. Boston, MA: Butterworths, 1989.

This dictionary provides a complete listing of over 2,500 terms in automotive engineering. It is not only a handy source for automotive experts but also a good reference for the general public. Not limited by country of origin, this dictionary provides the most currently used informal vocabularies, acronyms, abbreviations, and professional terminologies in the automotive engineering field.

560. Norback, Craig T., ed.   Chilton's complete book of
     automotive facts. Radnor, PA: Chilton Book Co., 1981.

     The Japanese transplant operations in America and the
     U.S. automobile industry in general are covered. The
     following areas are included in this volume: auto facts
     and statistics, auto repairs and maintenance, trucking
     industry, motorcycle industry, auto associations and
     clubs, auto safety, and auto publications.

561. SAE motor vehicle, safety, and environmental terminology.
     Warrendale, PA: Society of Automotive Engineers, 1977.

     This volume provides an alphabetical listing of motor
     vehicle, safety and environmental terminology commonly
     used as standards by the Society of Automotive Engineers.
     The major emphasis of this book is on auto safety
     measures.

562. Seale, J. N., compiler. Car service data. London ; New
     York, NY: Hamlyn Publishing Group, 1972.

     This book contains a compilation of data for over 1,100
     Japanese and foreign cars and light commercial vehicles
     from 1957 to 1972. The data cover engines, carburetion,
     ignition, electrical, transmission, and suspension items
     needed for general auto servicing and maintenance.

563. Wallace, A. compiler.   Automotive literature index,
     1947-1976. Toledo, OH: [s.n.], 1981.

     This index provides comprehensive coverage of the
     contents of three most popular automotive publications:
     Car and Driver, Motor Trend, and Road & Track from 1947
     to 1976. A complete listing of articles, photographs,
     announcements, tables, charts, road tests, book reviews,
     competition events, and statistics in all areas of
     automotive information from these three periodicals is
     included in this index.

564. Wherry, Joseph H.   Automobiles of the world.
     Philadelphia, PA: Chilton Book Co., 1968.

     This book illustrates the entire history of the
     automobile development with a collection of over 900 rare
     photographs of automobiles from all over the world. With
     global coverage in mind, the book highlights the most
     important developments in the history of automobiles,
     arranged geographically by country. Part one describes
     the evolution of automobiles.   Part two treats the
     automobile's infancy.   Part three covers the rise and
     fall of the steamers and electrics. Part four contains
     the automobile development of the early 20th century
     overseas, including the development of the Japanese
     automobile industry.   Part five details the history of
     American automobiles.

13

Audio-Visual Aids

565. <u>The American auto industry: current problems, possible future</u>. Washington, DC: National Public Radio, 1982. 1 sound cassette (79 min.): analog, stereo, 1 7/8 ips.

Originally broadcast in April 1902 on the National Public Radio program Morning Edition, this film reviews the history of the automobile industry, examines what has happened to the U.S. system of manufacture and why Japan is so competitive, and discusses the problems of labor relations, shop conditions, and underemployment.

566. <u>Automated assembly</u>. Dearborn, MI: Society of Manufacturing Engineers, 1987. 1 videocassette (34 min.): sound, color; 3/4 in.

This program describes the U.S. and Japanese automobile assembly-line operations and industrial developments.

567. <u>The Automobile: social and economic impact</u>. Tarrytown, NY: Associated Press; Distributed by Prentice-Hall Media, 1977. 2 filmstrips (230 fr.): color; 35 mm. + 2 sound discs + 1 guide.

The films examine ways in which the automobile affects the economic well-being of the nation, trace the history and sociological impact of the automobile, and project the possible future, particularly in light of environmental problems.

568. <u>Cars: how to buy a new or used car and keep it running (almost) forever</u>. Irvin, CA: Karl-Lorimar Home Video, 1986. 1 videocassette (VHS) (60 min.): sound, color; 1/2 in.

This program is one of the most comprehensive reports available for both domestic and foreign cars. It covers

topics such as what to look for in a new car, car
shopping and comparison, the road test, buying a good
used car, and car maintenance and repair techniques.

569. The Computer in the auto: systems and components. Mount
Krisco, NY: Vocational Media, 1985.   1 videocassette
(VHS) (65 min.): sound, color; 1/2 in.

Computer technology is commonly applied in Japanese and
American automobiles today. This film covers the basics
of the automotive computer, including integrated
circuits, fundamental system components, and other
automotive computer applications.

570. Coping with your car. McVey and Associates. Chicago,
IL: Distributed by Coronet Instructional Media, 1980. 4
rolls: color; 35 mm. + 4 cassettes (36 min. each) + 1
guide.

The program includes four parts : 1) Which car for you?,
2) Becoming the owner, 3) Keeping it running, and 4) Your
legal responsibilities. The accompanying guide is a good
resource for owners of either domestic or foreign cars.

571. Deming, William. [Deming, who turned Japanese automobile
manufacturing around in a news report by Marlene
Sanders]. [s.l.: s.n.], 1984. 1 sound tape reel (2
min.): 3 3/4 ips, mono.

Originally broadcast on CBS-TV on July 30, 1984, this
program contains an analysis of U.S. auto production
methods as compared to Japan's lean production system.
The emphasis of worker participation and quality control
in the U.S. auto industry is also discussed.

572. Factory--Hiroshima. Chicago, IL: Films Inc., 1979. 1
videocassette (VHS) (20 min.): sound, color; 1/2 in.

This video shows the work and family life of an assembly
line worker at the Mazda factory in Hiroshima, Japan.

573. Federal motor carrier safety regulations. United States
Bureau of Motor Carrier Safety.   Washington, DC:
Distributed by National Audiovisual Center, 1979.   514
slides: color; 2 x 2 in. + 8 cassettes and script.

These slides discuss federal motor carrier safety
regulations, including the qualifications of drivers,
inspection and maintenance of rigs, reporting and
recording accidents, permissible hours of service, and
transportation of hazardous materials. These regulations
affect both domestic and foreign cars in the United
States.

574. Front wheel drive: the concept, the fundamentals, the
operation.   Mount Krisco, NY: Vocational Media
Associates, 1989.   2 videocassettes (VHS) (40 min.):
sound, color; 1/2 in.

The origins of front-wheel-drive, how it compares to rear-wheel-drive, and the most common service repairs are offered in this program. The tapes provide information applicable to both domestic and foreign cars.

575. <u>Futureview: a look ahead</u>. Waukesha, WI: Burrus Research Associates, 1990. 6 soundcassettes: analog, 1 7/8 ips.

The latest trends in the technological development of the American and Japanese automobile industries are discussed.

576. <u>Golden age of the American automobile</u>. Los Angeles, CA: Increase Video, 1983. 1 videocassette (VHS) (55 min.): sound, color; 1/2 in.

The film celebrates American automobiles of the years 1919-1941. It includes archival photographs and films, with examples of some auto models. The program describes the development of many of today's engineering advances and the evolution of the early Japanese automobile industry.

577. <u>How to buy a vehicle: without being taken for a ride</u>. Minneapolis, MN: Shel-O'Brien Associates, 1989.   1 videocassette (VHS) (62 min.): sound, color; 1/2 in. + 1 guide.

This program is presented by a former car dealer who gives advice on test-driving a car, negotiating terms, and getting the best financing rate when deciding to buy a car. Suggestions and comments on shopping for an American or foreign-made car are also included.

578. <u>How to buy an automobile</u>. Kalamazoo, MI: Interpretive Education, 1978. 5 rolls (64 fr. each): color; 35 mm. + 3 cassettes (57 min.) + 1 guide.

Five parts are included in this program: costs, what to look for, new versus used cars, maintenance, and contracts and financing. The program is helpful for consumers considering either an American or a foreign-made car.

579. <u>Japan: a proper place in the world</u>. Northbrook, IL: Coronet Film & Video, 1987. 1 videocassette (57 min.): sound, color, with b&w sequences; 3/4 in. + 1 guide.

The program traces the fall of the Japanese empire and Japan's rapid rise since the end of World War II. Japan's importance in the automobile industry and trade is discussed.

580. <u>Japan: the Orient express</u>. [Indianapolis, IN]: Distributed by Christian Science Monitor, 1991.   1 videocassette (VHS) (60 min.): sound, color; 1/2 in.

Discusses the automobile industry in Japan and its trade

with other countries.   It also describes the postwar
economic and social conditions in Japan.

581. **Japan: toward the 21st century**.   Great Plains, NY: Great
     Plains National ITV, 1989.   2 videocassettes (60 min.):
     sound, color; 1/2 in.

     These videocassettes introduce aspects of Japanese
     culture, history, politics, and economics. They contain
     interviews with Japanese businessmen and officials who
     outline their goals for the turn of the century.

582. **Japanese approach to productivity**.   Detroit, MI:
     Automotive Industry Action Group, 1983. 4 videocassettes
     (240 min.): sound, color; 3/4 in.

     Defines the overall Japanese approach to labor
     productivity and discusses those issues applicable to the
     U.S. auto industry.

583. **Japanese car made in the U.S.A.**   Falls Church, VA:
     Landmark Films, 1987.   1 videocassette (VHS) (60 min.);
     sound, color, 1/2 in.

     Different work and management habits of Americans and
     Japanese are contrasted in this program that examines
     operations at New United Motor Manufacturing Inc., a
     joint venture between Toyota and General Motors in
     Fremont, California.

584. **Japanese cars, why are they so popular?** Chicago, IL:
     Encyclopedia Britannica Educational Corp., 1981.   1
     videocassette (VHS) (30 min.): sound, color; 1/2 in. + 1
     teacher's guide.

     Discusses the popularity of Japanese cars in foreign
     markets.

585. Lee, Albert.   **Call me Roger**.   Audio.   Chicago, IL:
     Nightingale-Conant Audio, 1988. 1 soundcassette: analog,
     stereo, 1 7/8 ips.

     The tape includes a history of the General Motors Corp.,
     the company's poor quality ratings, and its declining
     market shares in recent years. The company, located in
     Fremont, California, was replaced by New United Motors
     Manufacturing Inc., a joint venture between General
     Motors and Toyota.

586. **Made in Japan**. Lincoln, NE: GPN, 1978. 1 videocassette
     (VHS) (29 min.): sound, color; 1/2 in.

     The program explores the social, cultural, and
     psychological reasons for Japan's extraordinary
     industrial and commercial success since World War II. It
     emphasizes that while Japan lacks natural resources, its
     one great asset is its creative and hardworking people.
     The remarkable success of the Japanese automobile
     industry and trade is mentioned in this program.

587. **Made in Japan**.   Athens, GA: University of Georgia, Peabody Recording Center, 1981.   1 videocassette (VHS) (47 min.): sound, color; 1/2 in.

Traces the development of the Japanese automobile industry and discusses Japanese competition in the United States.

588. **Manufacturing miracles: a Japanese firm reinvents itself**. San Francisco, CA: California Newsreel, 1987.   1 videocassette (35 min.): sound, color; 3/4 in.

The program contrasts Japanese and American manufacturing and labor management systems, and discusses how the auto industry dealt with the economic recession and the gasoline shortage of 1974, with a major focus on the economic and technological performance of the Mazda Motor Corporation.   It shows how Mazda organized joint labor-management relationships throughout the firm and invested heavily in comprehensive training, eventually transforming itself into an integrated "team production system," while continually responding to the rapid-changing global economy.

589. **Me and my robot**.   Turner Broadcasting System.   Mount Kisco, NY: Distributed by Guidance Associates, 1988.   1 videocassette (VHS) (20 min.): sound, color; 1/2 in.

The program reviews current applications and possible future uses of robots, including their utilization in the automobile industry in the United States and Japan.

590. **Michigan at risk: the threat from Japan**.   Lansing, MI: Michigan Public Broadcasting, 1990.   1 videocassette (VHS) (27 min.): sound, color; 1/2 in.

Discusses U.S.-Japanese relations in the auto industry, including the negative impact of Japanese production on the American industry, the Japanese work ethic versus the American ethic, and Japanese production methods versus American methods.

591. **Postwar Japan: 40 years of economic recovery**.   NHK Enterprises.   Falls Church, VA: Distributed by Landmark Films, 1987.   1 videocassette (VHS) (60 min.): sound, color; 1/2 in.

The program reviews Japan's economic growth since World War II. The collapsed postwar economy is examined, and measures to increase productivity are shown.   It describes the basic structure of the Japanese economy and also mentions the automobile development that has earned Japan a major role in the global economy.

592. Quayle, Dan. **A member of the Senate Labor and Human Resources Committee defends the continuation of import quotas on Japanese automobiles: consumer advocate in rebuttal**. [s.l.: s.n., 1984].   1 sound tape reel (20 min.): 3 3/4 ips, mono.

This is a PBS program, broadcasted on May 2, 1984, concerning the debate between Senator Dan Qualye and Ralph Nader on the extension of the import quota imposed on Japanese automobiles. Current U.S.-Japanese auto trade relations and their future prospects are also discussed.

593. The Race for clean air. U.S. Environmental Protection Agency. Washington, DC: Distributed by National Audiovisual Center, 1975. 1 reel (27 min.): sound, color; 16 mm.

This motion picture shows the 1970 Clean Air Race, discusses the different control systems, fuels, and propulsion systems that were entered in the worldwide auto industry event.

594. The Road to perfection. [Los Angeles, CA: Released by Ruder, Finn & Rotman, 1986?]. 1 videocassette (VHS) (20 min.): sound, color; 1/2 in.

This program contains an overview of current events of the Mitsubishi Motors Corp., including the company's structure, research & development, manufacturing and quality control, and international activities.

595. The Shacho: a Japanese president and his company. Falls Church, VA: Landmark Films, 1987. 1 videocassette (VHS) (55 min.): sound, color, 1/2 in.

This program examines Japanese corporate management and organizational behavior. It explains how a company president in Japan has a role very different from his counterpart in the United States, in that he acts as a symbolic father figure to the extended family of workers.

596. A Test of Japanese management: Japanese cars made in the U.S.A.. Falls Church, VA: Landmark Films, 1987. 1 videocassette (VHS) (45 min.): sound, color; 1/2 in.

This program focuses on the joint venture of Toyota and General Motors established in Fremont, California. A documentary history of joint collaboration between these two companies to build the Chevy Nova is presented. American workers are shown as they spend three weeks in Japan and then in the Japanese-managed American auto plant as part of their orientation for working under Japanese culture. An analysis of Japanese management and labor relations as applied to the American autoworkers are covered.

597. Toyota. [Toyota City, Japan: Toyota Motor Corp., 1975?] 1 videocassette (VHS) (21 min.): sound, color; 1/2 in.

The program details the Japanese automobile assembly process from designing, manufacturing, and assembling, to completion, focusing on the Toyota auto plant. It also contains many promotional materials for Toyota automobiles.

598. **Transportation: the way ahead**.   United States Energy
     Research and Development Administration. Washington, DC:
     Distributed by National Audiovisual Center, 1979.   1
     videocassette (8 min.): sound, color; 3/4 in.

     The tape describes various ERDA (U.S. Energy Research and
     Development Administration) programs aimed at developing
     new fuel sources for automobiles, and discusses research
     being conducted with methanol, isopropanol, denatured
     alcohol, and other fuels not derived from petroleum.
     These programs will make a great impact on future auto
     development in Japan, the United States, and Europe.

599. **We are driven**.   Arlington, VA: Distributed by PBS Video,
     1984. 1 videocassette (VHS) (58 min.): sound, color; 1/2
     in.

     The video compares labor-management relations in Japan
     and the United States through an analysis of Nissan Motor
     Corp.'s facilities located in Tennessee and Japan.

600. **Wheels: the joy of cars**.   Beverly Hills, CA: Pacific Arts
     Home Video, 1988.   1 videocassette (VHS) (39 min.):
     sound, color; 1/2 in.

     This program traces the history and development of
     automobiles; looks at the dream and vintage cars of today
     and yesterday; explores the race track as cars become
     faster and more sophisticated; and follows the historic
     development in automotive craftsmanship, luxury and
     speed.

601. **Working in the automobile trade**.   Raybar Technical Films.
     Tarrytown, NY: Distributed by Prentice-Hall Media, 1977.
     4 rolls (240 fr.): color; 35 mm. + 4 cassettes (1/2
     track, mono, ca. 100 min.) + 1 guide.

     The film describes some of the job opportunities and
     careers in the automobile industry, and points out the
     specific skills needed both in performing the work
     satisfactorily and in developing a positive attitude
     which will lead to good customer, employer, and employee
     relationships.

Author and Editor Index

Adachi, Fumihiko, 91
Alster, Norm, 273
Anzai, Tatsuya, 411
Aoki, Doichi, 6, 7, 8
Armstrong, Larry, 274, 373, 442, 443, 478
Arnesen, Peter J., 150, 151, 374
Awanohara, Susumu, 377

Bagot, Brian, 153
Bairstow, Jeffrey, 337
Barrett, Amy, 444
Beauchamp, Marc, 497
Behar, Richard, 11
Berry, Bryan H., 275-77, 287
Bhaskar, Krish, 154
Bloomfield, Gerald T., 155, 156
Boger, Karl, 531, 532
Boroughs, Don L., 378
Borrus, Amy, 13, 379, 445
Boyer, Edward, 157
Bradley, Peter, 158
Bradsher, Keith, 380, 381
Brooke, Lindsay, 14, 15
Brown, Stuart F., 16
Browning, Robert J., 17, 159
Bryan, Michael F., 278
Bryant, Adam, 18, 160, 161
Bylinsky, Genei, 19
Byron, Christopher, 382

Calton, Jerry Merle, 383
Campbell, Harrison S., Jr., 310
Campbell, John Greighton, 338
Caplen, Brian, 446
Carroll, William, 557
Ceppos, Rich, 339, 384

Title Index

Subject Index

About the Compiler

SHEAU-YUEH J. CHAO is assistant professor and technical services librarian at Baruch College, City University of New York.